KOREA GRAMM for BEGINNE

A Complete Textbook and Work
Learn How to Read, Listen, and Write in Korean

Fluent in Korean

No part of this book including the audio material may be copied, reproduced, transmitted or distributed in any form without the prior written permission of the author. For permission requests, write to: support@fluentinkorean.com.

Also available:

Korean Short Stories for Beginners (https://geni.us/koreanstories)

Learn, Listen & Speak Korean (https://geni.us/koreanphrasebook)

TABLE OF CONTENTS

INTRODUCTION viii

LESSON 1: KOREAN ALPHABET SYSTEM – HANGUL 1

   TIME TO PRACTICE! 6
   QUICK RECAP 8

LESSON 2: DOUBLE CONSONANTS AND COMPOUND VOWELS 9

   TIME TO PRACTICE! 13
   QUICK RECAP 15

LESSON 3: SYLLABLE BLOCKS AND THE FINAL CONSONANT 16

   TIME TO PRACTICE! 24
   QUICK RECAP 29

LESSON 4: KOREAN PARTICLES – TOPIC MARKER AND SUBJECT MARKER EXPLAINED 30

   TIME TO PRACTICE! 36
   QUICK RECAP 39

LESSON 5: HOW TO INTRODUCE YOURSELF IN KOREAN 40

   TIME TO PRACTICE! 46
   QUICK RECAP 49

LESSON 6: HOW TO SAY THIS, THAT, HERE AND THERE – 이것/저것/그것 & 여기/저기/거기 50

   TIME TO PRACTICE! 57
   QUICK RECAP 60

LESSON 7: A BEGINNER'S GUIDE TO KOREAN NUMBERS 61

   TIME TO PRACTICE! 68
   QUICK RECAP 71

LESSON 8: MORE ON COUNTERS 72

   TIME TO PRACTICE! 76
   QUICK RECAP 79

LESSON 9: INTRODUCTION TO TIME, DAYS, WEEKS, AND MONTHS 80
TIME TO PRACTICE! 87
QUICK RECAP 89

LESSON 10: KOREAN TENSES – EXPRESSING THE PAST, PRESENT, AND FUTURE. 90
TIME TO PRACTICE! 98
QUICK RECAP 103

LESSON 11: AN EASY GUIDE TO KOREAN ADJECTIVES. 106
TIME TO PRACTICE! 113
QUICK RECAP 117

LESSON 12: SENTENCE STRUCTURE AND 좋다 VS. 좋아하다 118
TIME TO PRACTICE! 123
QUICK RECAP 126

LESSON 13: QUALIFIERS IN KOREAN 127
TIME TO PRACTICE! 133
QUICK RECAP 136

LESSON 14: THE MOST USEFUL ADVERBS 137
TIME TO PRACTICE! 144
QUICK RECAP 147

LESSON 15: PRESENT CONTINUOUS TENSE IN KOREAN 148
TIME TO PRACTICE! 152
QUICK RECAP 155

LESSON 16: RULES TO TURN VERBS INTO NOUNS/GERUNDS 156
TIME TO PRACTICE! 161
QUICK RECAP 165

LESSON 17: INTRODUCTION TO KOREAN CONJUNCTIONS. 166
TIME TO PRACTICE! 172
QUICK RECAP 176

LESSON 18: WHO, WHAT, WHEN, WHERE, WHY, AND HOW 177
TIME TO PRACTICE! 183
QUICK RECAP 186

LESSON 19: LOCATION MARKERS -에/-에서 187

TIME TO PRACTICE! 191
QUICK RECAP 195

LESSON 20: HOW TO USE KOREAN POSTPOSITIONS "FROM" AND "UNTIL" 196

TIME TO PRACTICE! 202
QUICK RECAP 206

LESSON 21: HOW TO MAKE AN IMPERATIVE SENTENCE 207

TIME TO PRACTICE! 210
QUICK RECAP 213

CONCLUSION 214

ENGLISH-KOREAN GLOSSARY 215

APPENDIX-SOUND CHANGE RULES 218

HOW TO DOWNLOAD THE FREE AUDIO FILES 221

ABOUT THE AUTHOR 223

$8 FREE BONUSES

Scan the QR code below to claim your bonuses.

OR

 Visit the link below:

https://fluentinkorean.com/grammar-bonus/

INTRODUCTION

When learning any language, grammar definitely comes up as the most challenging – and boring – part. Korean is no different. Unfortunately, grammar is not something that can just be brushed off as an afterthought.

You simply cannot skip learning grammar if you truly want to become proficient. It doesn't work that way, and there are no shortcuts. If you want to be able to express yourself in Korean using clear and precise language, you need to build a strong foundation in Korean grammar.

This book is here to help you. In the lessons in this book, we will lay out the rules of Korean grammar and provide you with lots of examples, explanations, and exercises.

Practice Your Korean Listening Skills and Pronunciation

A key to success in language learning is to get a good grasp of pronunciation at the beginning of your lessons. This requires constant listening practice.
With this book's audio accompaniment, you will get a head start in your listening comprehension as well as hone your pronunciation straight off the bat.

Each lesson contains audio narrated by a native Korean speaker.

By listening to the audio and reading the written text at the same time, you will be able to connect how a word or sentence looks with how it sounds when spoken in actual Korean conversations.

Important note: The link to download the audio files is available at the end of this book. (Page 221)

Embedded Grammar Workbook

There is no need to buy a separate workbook to help you practice the grammar points you learn. We have integrated hundreds of different exercises into the book. This way, you will be able to cement your learning through taking the quizzes after each grammar lesson, and you will be able to assess your progress as you go along.

Important note: The answer key for each exercise is provided at the end of the lesson.

Build Learning Habits

This book also aims to help you build learning habits that will help you sustain learning Korean even if your motivation wanes as you go along. You'll find that the book is divided into 21 lessons with one lesson meant to be tackled each day. After 21 days of studying consistently every day, you will have formed learning habits that will ultimately help you achieve your learning goals.

Korean Grammar, Simplified

Korean grammar is already complicated – we don't need to make it any more complex. So in this book, you'll notice that we use the simplest yet thorough explanations. We do not want to burden you with wordy explanations and unnecessary jargon. Instead, in this book we explain Korean grammar in a way that makes it easily digestible and easy to grasp.

We have put a lot of effort into designing this book in a way that will be most useful to your Korean language learning journey. We certainly hope that it will help you build the strong grammar foundation you need to eventually reach fluency in Korean.

Thank you very much and good luck.

Fluent in Korean Team

PLEASE READ!

 The link to download the audio files is available at the end of this book. (Page 221)

 The answer key for each exercise is provided at the end of the lesson.

LESSON 1: KOREAN ALPHABET SYSTEM – HANGUL

For those of you who have never been exposed to the Korean written language, the Korean alphabet is actually very easy to learn. We are confident that you will be able to at least read (phonetically) simple Korean words by the end of this lesson.

Are you up for the challenge?

A Bit of History

Did you know that the Korean alphabet is less than 600 years old? Before it was created, the Koreans had to rely on Chinese characters for their written language. Because the Chinese characters were extremely difficult to learn, it was only the elite who could read and write. This left most of the common folk, who were mostly farmers, illiterate.

In 1446, King Sejong the Great, one of the most revered kings in Korean history, gathered together the country's best linguists and led the creation of the phonetic alphabet called Hangul (also spelled Hangeul). An interesting fact is that each character of Hangul was modeled after the shape of the mouth when making the corresponding sounds.

Hangul Day is celebrated every year in October in South Korea to commemorate the significance of what King Sejong achieved. Hangul is recognized among the world's linguists as the most logical writing system.

King Sejong's sole purpose was to create a written language that is easy for even the commonest of people to learn quickly. He wanted to wipe out illiteracy throughout the country.

Knowing all that, there's no reason why any non-Korean cannot learn just as quickly, right?

Hangul (Korean Alphabet System)

Hangul is made up of 14 consonants and 10 vowels. King Sejong believed that with these 24 characters, along with an additional 16 that are derived from combining some of the first 24, there was not a human sound that could not be written. Or so he thought.

It turns out that there are actually a few sounds that cannot be written in Hangul, such as the sounds of F, V, and Z from the English alphabet. But the Korean language itself does not have any words with those sounds, so I guess we have to give him a pass on that.

Here are the 24 basic characters in Hangul:

Consonants

ㄱ	ㄴ	ㄷ	ㄹ	ㅁ	ㅂ	ㅅ
ㅇ	ㅈ	ㅊ	ㅋ	ㅌ	ㅍ	ㅎ

Vowels

ㅏ	ㅑ	ㅓ	ㅕ	ㅗ
ㅛ	ㅜ	ㅠ	ㅡ	ㅣ

That's it! All you need to do is know the sounds of these characters, and you are on your way to reading and writing in Korean! Of course, there are those 16 extra ones that are combinations of two or more of these first 24, but let's first start with the basics.

Here are the consonants:

Listen to Track 1

Consonant	Sound		Consonant	Sound
ㄱ	g (*girl*)		ㅇ	silent

2

ㄴ	n (*name*)	ㅈ	j (*joy*)
ㄷ	d (*dog*)	ㅊ	ch (*cherry*)
ㄹ	r / l (*later*)	ㅋ	k (*cake*)
ㅁ	m (*mother*)	ㅌ	t (*tomato*)
ㅂ	b (*boy*)	ㅍ	p (*puppy*)
ㅅ	s (*snow*)	ㅎ	h (*hello*)

Note: The consonant "ㅇ" is the silent consonant that is used when a syllable in a word has only a vowel sound, such as "ah" or "oh." In Korean, you cannot use a vowel alone without a consonant, so there is the silent consonant. It also has the pronunciation "ng" (as in hu**ng**) when used as a final consonant, more on final consonants later.

One of the things that most English speakers have trouble pronouncing is the "ㄹ." It's neither the sound of L nor R – it's somewhere in the middle. Think of it as closer to a trilled R – you want to feel your tongue touch the roof of your mouth quickly when pronouncing this consonant. Almost like how the "t" in the American pronunciation of the words "otter," "butter," and "later" feels! Keep this in mind whenever you see the consonant "ㄹ."

And now the vowels:

Listen to Track 2

Vowel	Sound	Vowel	Sound
ㅏ	ah (*all*)	ㅛ	yo (*yogurt*)
ㅑ	yah (*yard*)	ㅜ	ooh (*moon*)

ㅓ	uh *(undo)*	ㅠ	yu *(you)*
ㅕ	yuh *(yum)*	─	eu *(ew)*
ㅗ	oh *(over)*	ㅣ	ee *(eel)*

All vowels are made from adding more lines to the two stem vowels (─, ㅣ).

Notice that among these vowels, there are vowels that are vertical (ㅏ, ㅑ, ㅓ, ㅕ, ㅣ) and vowels that are horizontal (ㅗ, ㅛ, ㅜ, ㅠ, ─). You need to remember when combining: **Vertical** vowels are added to the **right** of the consonant, and the **horizontal** vowels are added **below** the consonant.

Another thing to note about the vowels: When there are two smaller lines connected to the longer line (ㅑ, ㅕ, ㅛ, ㅠ), they all have a "y" sound in the pronunciation – yah, yah, yuh, yo, yu.

Let's try combining the consonants and vowels:

Listen to Track 3

ㄱ + ㅏ = 가	[g + ah = gah]
ㄴ + ㅏ = 나	[n + ah = nah]
ㄷ + ㅗ = 도	[d + oh = doh]
ㅂ + ㅣ = 비	[b + ee = bee]
ㅇ + ㅜ = 우	[silent + ooh = ooh]

In this manner, you can write numerous Korean words with the basic 24 characters.

Let's try reading some simple Korean words:

Listen to Track 4

우유	[oo-yoo] *milk*
다리	[dah-rhee] *leg*
나비	[nah-bee] *butterfly*
기차	[gee-cha] *train*
오이	[oh-ee] *cucumber*

See how easy that was?

Practice

Now, let's see if you can try to pronounce the following few words without romanization. Feel free to refer to the charts above:

Listen to Track 5

- 구두 *dress shoes*
- 두부 *tofu*
- 여우 *fox*
- 포도 *grapes*
- 사자 *lion*

TIME TO PRACTICE!

Korean Alphabet System – Hangul

Exercise 1. Fill in the blanks to complete the following table:

Consonant	Sound	Consonant	Sound
ㄱ	1. _____	ㅇ	Silent
ㄴ	N	ㅈ	J
ㄷ	2. _____	ㅊ	6. _____
ㄹ	R / L	ㅋ	7. _____
ㅁ	3. _____	ㅌ	8. _____
ㅂ	4. _____	ㅍ	9. _____
ㅅ	5. _____	ㅎ	10. _____

Exercise 2. Fill in the blanks to complete the following table:

Vowel	Sound	Vowel	Sound
ㅏ	1. _____	ㅗ	4. _____
ㅑ	2. _____	ㅜ	ooh (u)
ㅓ	uh (eo)	ㅠ	5. _____
ㅕ	yuh (yeo)	ㅡ	6. _____
ㅗ	3. _____	ㅣ	7. _____

Exercise 3. Determine if the following vowels are Vertical / Horizontal:

1. ㅏ : [Vertical / Horizontal]
2. ㅗ : [Vertical / Horizontal]
3. ㅑ : [Vertical / Horizontal]
4. ㅜ : [Vertical / Horizontal]
5. ㅓ : [Vertical / Horizontal]
6. ㅠ : [Vertical / Horizontal]
7. ㅕ : [Vertical / Horizontal]
8. ㅡ : [Vertical / Horizontal]
9. ㅗ : [Vertical / Horizontal]
10. ㅣ : [Vertical / Horizontal]

Exercise 4. Determine if the following characters are Vowel / Consonant:

1. ㄱ : [Vowel / Consonant]
2. ㅊ : [Vowel / Consonant]
3. ㅇ : [Vowel / Consonant]
4. ㅏ : [Vowel / Consonant]

5. ㄴ : [Vowel / Consonant]

6. ㅕ : [Vowel / Consonant]

7. ㅈ : [Vowel / Consonant]

8. ㅁ : [Vowel / Consonant]

9. ㄷ : [Vowel / Consonant]

10. ㅌ : [Vowel / Consonant]

Exercise 5. Determine if the following statements are True / False:

1. Vertical vowels are added to the left of the consonant. [True / False]
2. The consonant "ㄹ" and "L" are pronounced the same. [True / False]
3. The consonant "ㄹ" and "R" are pronounced the same. [True / False]
4. The character "ㅇ" is the silent vowel. [True / False]
5. There are 10 basic vowels in Korean. [True / False]
6. There are 14 basic consonants in Korean. [True / False]
7. Horizontal vowels are added below the consonant. [True / False]

ANSWERS:

Exercise 1

1. G / 2. D / 3. M / 4. B / 5. S / 6. Ch / 7. K / 8. T / 9. P / 10. H

Exercise 2

1. ah (a) / 2. yah (ya) / 3. oh (o) / 4. yo / 5. yu / 6. eu / 7. ee (i)

Exercise 3

1. Vertical / 2. Horizontal / 3. Vertical / 4. Horizontal / 5. Vertical / 6. Horizontal / 7. Vertical / 8. Horizontal / 9. Horizontal / 10. Vertical

Exercise 4

1. Consonant / 2. Consonant / 3. Consonant / 4. Vowel / 5. Consonant / 6. Vowel / 7. Consonant / 8. Consonant / 9. Consonant / 10. Consonant

Exercise 5

1. False: Vertical vowels are added to the right of the consonant. / 2. False: The pronunciation of "L" and "ㄹ" are different. / 3. False: The pronunciation of "R" and "ㄹ" are different. / 4. False "ㅇ" is the silent consonant. / 5. True / 6. True / 7. True

QUICK RECAP

There you go! You can now read basic Korean (at least phonetically).

The Korean alphabet system called Hangul (or Hangeul) consists of a set of consonants and a set of vowels that are combined to form phonetic syllables. We have covered the fundamental part of the alphabet (14 consonants and 10 vowels) in this lesson, and you can now recognize and pronounce simple syllables.

In the next lesson, we will go over the additional 16 characters in the alphabet. If you practice and become familiar with the ones we have already covered, learning the others will be much easier for you. Once you learn the entire alphabet, you will be able to phonetically read anything in Korean.

Comprehension will come later as you learn more vocabulary and grammar.

Learning a new language is not an easy task. It requires will and dedication. Or you could just move to Korea and live there for about two years, interacting with people who speak no English.

When learning a new language, you need to be diligent about practicing every single day. We always say that the three most important things you need to do to retain what you learn are:

1. Repetition

2. Repetition

3. Repetition

And take advantage of every opportunity to *hear* the language spoken. Watch K-dramas. Listen to K-pop. As you learn more, try to pick out the words that you recognize when you hear them. Try to mimic what they say and how they say it.

We're confident that with just a little effort to practice and review every day, you will progress quickly! Be patient and gradually increase your vocabulary. We're rooting for you!

LESSON 2: DOUBLE CONSONANTS AND COMPOUND VOWELS

In this lesson, we will continue with additional characters that are created by combining the basic ones. As a review, here are the basic 14 consonants and 10 vowels:

Listen to Track 6

- **Consonants:** ㄱ ㄴ ㄷ ㄹ ㅁ ㅂ ㅅ ㅇ ㅈ ㅊ ㅋ ㅌ ㅍ ㅎ
- **Vowels:** ㅏ ㅑ ㅓ ㅕ ㅗ ㅛ ㅜ ㅠ ㅡ ㅣ

Assuming that you are already familiar with the first 24 characters, we will now move on to the double consonants and compound vowels, which make up an additional 16 characters (5 consonants and 11 vowels).

Double Consonants

Before we go over the following consonants, we need to let you know that the Korean consonants are divided into three types of sounds: **plain, aspirated,** and **tense**. Plain consonants are pronounced regularly like consonants in English. Aspirated consonants are said with a burst of air — like the difference between the aspirated "t" in "tore," and the plain "t" in "store." Tense consonants are harsher and stiffer than plain consonants, with more time spent on them during pronunciation. We will be explaining that further in a later lesson; but for now, we just want you to be aware that the double consonants have **tense** sounds.

Listen to Track 7

Consonant	Romanization	Notes
ㄲ	gg	Similar sound to the "k" in the word "sky" or "c" in the word "ricochet." Also, the sound of the "q" in Spanish "que."

ㄸ	dd	Similar sound to the "t" in the word "store," or the sound that "t" and "d" make together in "hotdog."
ㅃ	bb	Similar sound to the "p" in the word "spa," or the sound of the "p" in Spanish "¿qué pasa?"
ㅆ	sc	Similar sound to the "s" in the word "sit," the "c" in "cent," and "sc" in "science." Many English words with "s," "c," or "sc" have similar *tense* pronunciation. The "ㅆ" is much easier for English speakers to pronounce than the single consonant "ㅅ."
ㅉ	jj	We cannot think of a single English word that has this sound. This is a sound that "t" at the end of a word and "j" at the beginning of the next word would make together, like "hot June" or "get juice."

Whew! We hope you get the general idea. Don't get overwhelmed or discouraged, because *everyone* struggles with the pronunciation. You will get better as you practice. It may feel silly, but keep trying to vocalize the sounds out loud. No one will make fun of you!

Now, let's move on to the rest of the vowels.

Compound Vowels

Listen to Track 8

Vowel	Romanization	Notes
ㅐ	ae	Sounds like "a" in "cat."
ㅔ	eh	Sounds like "e" in "pet," but in conversation, there is not much distinction between words with "ㅐ" and words with "ㅔ."
ㅒ	yea	Sounds like "a" in "yak." Remember that the two smaller lines indicate a "y" sound.
ㅖ	ye	Sounds like "e" in "yes." Again, not much distinction between "ㅒ" and "ㅖ."

와	wah	ㅗ [oh] + ㅏ [ah] = 와 [wah]
외	weh	ㅗ [oh] + ㅣ [ee] = 외 [oi]? No... it is actually pronounced [weh]. This is the only diphthong that does not make logical sense.
왜	wae	ㅗ [oh] + ㅐ [ae] = 왜 [wea]
워	wuh	ㅜ [ooh] + ㅓ [uh] = 워 [wuh]
웨	weh	ㅜ [ooh] + ㅔ [eh] = 웨 [weh]
위	wee	ㅜ [ooh] + ㅣ [ee] = 위 [wee]
의	eui	─ [eu] + ㅣ [ee] = 의 [eui]

That's it! Now you have been introduced to the entire Hangul alphabet. Let's now see the alphabet in action!

Word Practice

We still have to cover syllable blocks, but already you can write **so many** words with what we have learned so far. You can begin to build your vocabulary starting today!

Keep in mind that the romanization is just for reference and may not be the *exact* pronunciation of the words. After you have memorized all the sounds in the Hangul alphabet, you should get used to reading Hangul without romanization.

Let's now look at some words:

• **People**

Listen to Track 9

Word	Romanization	Definition
아빠	ap-pa	*dad*
오빠	op-pa	*older brother (to a female)*
누나	nooh-nah	*older sister (to a male)*

이모	ee-mo	aunt (maternal)
고모	go-mo	aunt (paternal)
의사	eui-sa	medical doctor
가수	gah-soo	singer

- **Body Parts**

Listen to Track 10

Word	Romanization	Definition
코	koh	nose
다리	dah-rhee (sounds like American pronunciation of "dotty")	leg
머리	muh-ree (sounds like American pronunciation of "muddy")	head
귀	gwee	ear

- **Food**

Listen to Track 11

Word	Romanization	Definition
고기	go-ghee	meat
소고기	so-go-ghee	소 (cow) + 고기 (meat) = 소고기 (beef)
돼지고기	dweh-ji-go-ghee	돼지 (pig) + 고기 (meat) = 돼지고기 (pork)
포도	poh-doh	grapes
사과	sah-gwah	apple
오이	oh-ee	cucumber
두부	doo-boo	tofu
치즈	chee-jeu	cheese
차	cha	tea
커피	kuh-pee	coffee
우유	oo-yoo	milk
과자	gwah-ja	snack(s)

TIME TO PRACTICE!

Double Consonants and Compound Vowels

Exercise 1. Fill in the blanks to complete the following table:

Single Consonant	Double Consonant	Sound
1. _____	ㄲ	2. _____
ㄷ	3. _____	dd
4. _____	ㅆ	5. _____
ㅈ	6. _____	jj

Exercise 2. Fill in the blanks to complete the following table:

Vowel 1	Vowel 2	Compound Vowel	Sound
1. _____	ㅏ	ㅘ	2. _____
ㅗ	3. _____	ㅚ	weh (oe)
ㅗ	ㅐ	4. _____	wae
5. _____	ㅓ	ㅝ	6. _____
ㅜ	7. _____	ㅞ	weh (we)
ㅜ	ㅣ	8. _____	wee (wi)
9. _____	ㅣ	ㅢ	10. _____

Exercise 3. Determine if the following vowels are Basic / Compound:

1. ㅐ : [Basic / Compound]
2. ㅡ : [Basic / Compound]
3. ㅣ : [Basic / Compound]
4. ㅔ : [Basic / Compound]
5. ㅗ : [Basic / Compound]

6. ㅜ : [Basic / Compound]
7. ㅓ : [Basic / Compound]
8. ㅐ : [Basic / Compound]
9. ㅏ : [Basic / Compound]
10. ㅖ : [Basic / Compound]

Exercise 4. Determine if the following combinations are Correct / Incorrect:

1. ㄱ + ㄱ = ㅋ [Correct / Incorrect]
2. ㅈ + ㅈ = ㅉ [Correct / Incorrect]
3. ㅗ + ㅐ = ㅙ [Correct / Incorrect]

4. ㄷ + ㄷ = ㅌ [Correct / Incorrect]
5. ㅗ + ㅣ = ㅢ [Correct / Incorrect]
6. ㅅ + ㅅ = ㅆ [Correct / Incorrect]

7. ㅂ + ㅂ = ㅃ [Correct / Incorrect]   9. ㅜ + ㅣ = ㅐ [Correct / Incorrect]

8. ㅡ + ㅣ = ㅜ [Correct / Incorrect]   10. ㅗ + ㅏ = ㅘ [Correct / Incorrect]

Exercise 5. Determine if the following statements are True / False:

1. A compound vowel consists of 3 vowels. [True / False]
2. There are 5 double consonants in Korean. [True / False]
3. There is no difference in pronunciation between single and double consonants. [True / False]
4. There are 11 compound vowels in Korean. [True / False]
5. Double consonants have aspirated sounds. [True / False]

ANSWERS:

Exercise 1

1. ㄱ / 2. gg / 3. ㄸ / 4. ㅅ / 5. sc / 6. ㅉ

Exercise 2

1. ㅗ / 2. wah (wa) / 3. ㅣ / 4. ㅙ / 5. ㅜ / 6. wuh (wo) / 7. ㅖ / 8. ㅟ / 9. ㅡ / 10. eui (ui)

Exercise 3

1. Compound / 2. Basic / 3. Basic / 4. Compound / 5. Basic / 6. Basic / 7. Basic / 8. Compound / 9. Basic / 10. Compound

Exercise 4

1. Incorrect / 2. Correct / 3. Correct / 4. Incorrect / 5. Incorrect / 6. Correct / 7. Correct / 8. Incorrect / 9. Incorrect / 10. Correct

Exercise 5

1. False: Compound vowel consists of 2 vowels. / 2. True / 3. False: Double consonants have more tensed sounds than single consonants. / 4. True / 5. False: Double consonants have tensed sounds.

QUICK RECAP

In this lesson, we covered the double consonants and compound vowels to add to the 24 characters that we have already learned in the previous lesson.

- **14 basic consonants + 5 double consonants = 19 total consonants**
- **10 basic vowels + 11 compound vowels = 21 total vowels**

In the next lesson, we will be explaining the final consonant. The final consonant is added at the end (bottom) of the syllable. Then we will finally be ready to start learning some grammar and be on our way to writing simple sentences!

LESSON 3: SYLLABLE BLOCKS AND THE FINAL CONSONANT

In this lesson, we will be looking at the literal building blocks of the Korean language, syllable blocks, as well as how to use final consonants at the end of syllable blocks. We felt this was a good place to introduce the syllable blocks, because it is important to know how the consonants and vowels are put together to form Korean syllables.

Keeping in mind that we are learning a language that is so different from the languages that use the Roman alphabet, we have to talk about how the characters physically come together to make words.

Rather than writing the characters in a linear chain, the Hangul characters are grouped together by syllable. Hangul is *phonetically written*, and *each syllable gets assigned a block*. We call this a **syllable block**. A syllable block is made up of two or more characters to make one syllable. And every word is made up of one or more syllable blocks.

There are nine possible types of syllable blocks, but the last one is rarely used. (Please don't get overwhelmed. We assure you it looks more complicated than it actually is.)

1. Consonant + Vertical Vowel
2. Consonant + Horizontal Vowel
3. Consonant + Compound Vowel
4. Consonant + Vertical Vowel + Final Consonant
5. Consonant + Horizontal Vowel + Final Consonant
6. Consonant + Compound Vowel + Final Consonant
7. Consonant + Vertical Vowel + (Final Consonant + Final Consonant)
8. Consonant + Horizontal Vowel + (Final Consonant + Final Consonant)
9. Consonant + Compound Vowel + (Final Consonant + Final Consonant)

Let's take a look at the first three types of syllable blocks:

- **Syllable blocks: Consonant + Vowel**

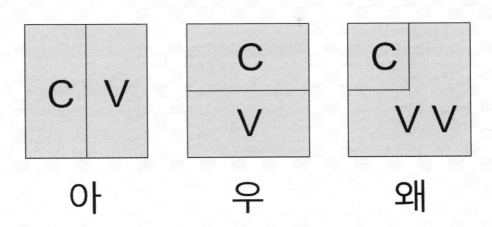

These are the simplest blocks to use. They only consist of one consonant and one vowel. The third syllable block here consists of one consonant and a compound vowel, which we learned about in the last lesson!

The next types of syllable blocks will introduce a new player in the game, the final consonant!

The Final Consonant

The final consonant is the last thing added to the syllable block. The final consonant in a syllable is called 받침 [baht-chim], which literally means "support from underneath." Knowing how to accurately utilize this feature of Korean writing is super important! The final consonant and its use, or absence, from a syllable will inform you which version of particles/endings to use. The final consonant can also carry over sounds* to neighboring syllables, and knowing how to read things smoothly will make you sound more natural when speaking!

| Note: | For information on the final consonant and how it affects neighboring syllables, please reference the Appendix - Sound Change Rules section at the end of this book. |

Let's take a look at the next types of syllable blocks:

- **Syllable blocks: Consonant + Vowel + Final Consonant**

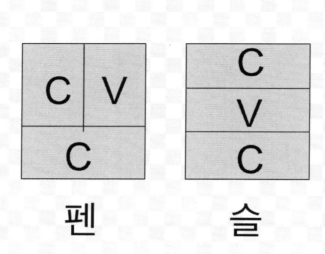

Listen to Track 12

Let's look at the English word "pencil" phonetically written in Korean above. Written in Hangul, the word "pencil" will look like this: 펜슬.

Both syllables end with a consonant. The "n" (ㄴ) will be added at the bottom of the first syllable, and the "l" (ㄹ) will be added at the bottom of the second syllable.

- **Syllable blocks: Consonant + Compound Vowel + Final Consonant**

The next syllable block represents syllables that have the consonant + compound vowel + consonant pattern. An example is the word 원 [won], which is the South Korean currency.

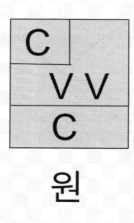

This is another relatively simple syllable block! You might run into trouble when trying to remember the layering of the compound vowels and how to connect them to the final consonant. Keep referring to the charts we provided in the previous lesson, practice writing them often. Remember, repetition is key!

- **Syllable blocks: Consonant + Vowel + 2 Final Consonants**

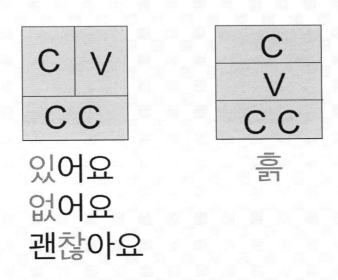

The last syllable blocks represent the syllables that end with two consonants, which include the double consonants that we have learned. Some of the words that have syllables ending with two consonants are:

Listen to Track 13

- 밖 **[bahk]** - means _"outside"_
- 있어요 **[is-suh-yo]** - means _"does exist"_ or _"have"_
- 없어요 **[up-suh-yo]** - means _"does not exist"_ or _"have not"_
- 괜찮아요 **[gwen-cha-nah-yo]** - means _"it's okay," "I'm okay,"_ or _"No thank you"_
- 흙 **[heuk]** - means _"dirt"_ or _"soil"_

As you will notice, there is no example shown for the last syllable block. That is because although it is theoretically possible to have a syllable constructed this way, it is very rarely used. In fact, we could not find a Korean syllable using this structure.

When you see written Korean words or when you are writing your own words, you should keep these syllable blocks in mind and recognize how the shapes of the characters change slightly in order to keep the size of the syllables uniform.

Once you've gotten some practice under your belt with writing the Korean words, this pattern will become second nature to you. Of course, if your writing is mainly on the keyboard or on your mobile device, the adjustments are automatically made for you. Isn't technology great?

Reminder about Korean consonants:

The consonants can be grouped into three different types of sounds: *plain*, *aspirated*, and *tense.* In the table below, I will use the vowel ㅏ [ah] with all the consonants so you can read them out loud.

Plain consonants are regular consonants, aspirated consonants have a burst of air when you say them, and you linger on the sound a bit longer on tense consonants.

Notice that ㄱ, ㄷ, ㅂ, and ㅈ have both *aspirated* and *tense* counterparts, while ㅅ has the *tense* counterpart ㅆ, and ㅇ has the *aspirated* counterpart ㅎ.

Listen to Track 14

Plain	가	나	다	라	마	바	사	아	자
Aspirated	카		타			파		하	차
Tense	까		따			빠	싸		짜

Fun fact: The shape of all Korean vowels and consonants mimics the shape of the mouth when pronouncing each letter. The ones that are easiest to recognize are the labial consonants ㅁ, ㅂ, ㅃ, ㅍ. The shapes of all these are closed because you need to close your lips first before making their sounds.

You will need to train your ears to *hear* the sound differences when listening, as well as pay close attention to the pronunciation differences when speaking.

Listen to Track 15

- 가 **[gah]** - Tongue and throat relaxed (like the sound "ga" in *Ghandi*)
- 카 **[ka]** - Throat opens and expels air (like the sound "ca" in *car*)
- 까 **[kka]** - Throat closed and back of the tongue tense (like the sound "k" in *sky* or *scar*)

Repeat these three sounds over and over, paying attention to what your mouth is doing when you say them and what the differences are. Then apply the same concept to the rest of the consonants in the table.

The goal is not to make you sound like a native, because that is very difficult to do when you learn a second language. But you still need to learn to distinguish between all the different sounds in order to understand and to be understood when communicating.

Listen to Track 16

For example, the word 사다 means "to buy," whereas the word 싸다 means "to be cheap." Can you see how someone could be completely misunderstood when the listener cannot hear the word clearly? You can expect similar emphasis on pronunciation in all of the lessons in this book. Stick with us, and your pronunciation skills will be the envy of all of your Korean-learning friends!

In our experience, English speakers don't seem to have as much trouble with the aspirated sounds, but they often have difficulty differentiating between *plain* and *tense* consonants.

Hangul Wrap-up

You now have all the information you need to write any word in Korean, as well as to phonetically sound out any single syllable block. You do have to apply some additional pronunciation rules when you read words with two or more syllables or when you are reading a sentence, but we will cover that as we go.

• Writing

One thing that we need to mention about writing Hangul is that all strokes should be written from left to right and from top to bottom.

If you want to practice writing Hangul as well as learn the proper sounds, there is a great app you can download to your mobile device. It is made by the Language Education Institute at Seoul National University. The app guides you through the proper stroke order and pronunciation and includes tests for you to see your progress.

Go ahead! Give it a try! SNU LEI App for Android , SNU LEI App for Apple iOS

• Typing

If you haven't done it already, you should think about installing the Korean Hangul keyboard on your computer and your mobile devices.

Keep in mind that on a Korean keyboard:

- o The consonants are on the left half of the keyboard.
- o The vowels are on the right half of the keyboard.

- o The shift key will give you the five double consonants and two vowels ㅐ and ㅖ.
- o You can get the compound vowels by consecutively typing the two vowels that make up the particular compound vowel you want.

Once you have mastered the keyboard, you will be able to use more study references online, such as the <u>Naver Korean Dictionary</u>. It is a good resource for learning and verifying correct pronunciation of words.

Word Practice

Now that we are able to read and write more words, let's add some words to our vocabulary.

In lesson two, we learned some words in the categories of people, body parts, and food. Now that we have learned how to add final consonants, we can make the lists more comprehensive (some words are repeated). But I will not overwhelm you with too many. We will learn more in future lessons.

- • **Immediate Family**

Listen to Track 17

Word	Romanization	Definition
엄마	um-ma	*mom*
아빠	ap-pa	*dad*
오빠	op-pa	*older brother (to a female)*
언니	un-nee	*older sister (to a female)*
형	hyung	*older brother (to a male)*
누나	nooh-nah	*older sister (to a male)*
동생	dong-saeng	*younger sibling*
남동생	nahm-dong-saeng	*younger brother*
여동생	yuh-dong-saeng	*younger sister*

Mini Quiz: *Notice that 동생 is younger sibling, 남동생 is younger brother, and 여동생 is younger sister. What do you think the words for male and female are? Any guesses? Yes! You're correct! 남 is male and 여 is female (adjectives). The words for "man" and "woman" are* **남**자 *(male person) and* **여**자 *(female person).*

- **Body Parts**

Listen to Track 18

Word	Romanization	Definition
머리	muh-ree (sounds like American pronunciation of "muddy")	*head*
얼굴	eol-gool (this is nearly impossible to romanize)	*face*
눈	noon	*eye(s)*
코	koh	*nose*
입	eep	*mouth (sometimes lips)*
입술	eep-sool	*lips*
귀	gwee	*ear(s)*

Fun Homework!

You might be familiar with the popular song "눈, 코, 입" (*Eyes, Nose, Lips*) by Taeyang (태양) from the K-pop group **Big Bang**. Listen to it and see if you can pick out those three words in the song.

TIME TO PRACTICE!

A. Syllable Blocks

Exercise 1. Write down the number of consonants for the following words:

Example: 땅 (*Ground*): 2 (ㄸ, ㅇ) / 흙 (*Soil*): 3 (ㅎ, ㄹ, ㄱ)

1. 각 (*Angle*): _____
2. 간 (*Liver*): _____
3. 금 (*Gold*): _____
4. 곰 (*Bear*): _____
5. 띠 (*Belt*): _____

6. 값 (*Value*): _____
7. 넋 (*Soul*): _____
8. 반 (*Half*): _____
9. 사 (*Four*): _____
10. 탑 (*Tower*): _____

Exercise 2. Determine if the vowels in the words are Basic / Compound (Complex):

1. 형 (*Older brother to a male*): [Basic / Compound (Complex)]
2. 팔 (*Arm*): [Basic / Compound (Complex)]
3. 폐 (*Lung*): [Basic / Compound (Complex)]
4. 턱 (*Chin*): [Basic / Compound (Complex)]
5. 털 (*Hair*): [Basic / Compound (Complex)]
6. 통 (*Barrel*): [Basic / Compound (Complex)]
7. 틈 (*Crack*): [Basic / Compound (Complex)]
8. 칼 (*Knife*): [Basic / Compound (Complex)]
9. 체 (*Filter*): [Basic / Compound (Complex)]
10. 쥐 (*Rat*): [Basic / Compound]

Exercise 3. Determine if the vowels in the following words are Horizontal / Vertical:

1. 덫 (*Trap*): [Horizontal / Vertical]
2. 동 (*Copper*): [Horizontal / Vertical]
3. 등 (*Back*): [Horizontal / Vertical]
4. 딸 (*Daughter*): [Horizontal / Vertical]
5. 뜻 (*Meaning*): [Horizontal / Vertical]

6. 맛 (*Taste*): [Horizontal / Vertical]
7. 면 (*Cotton*): [Horizontal / Vertical]
8. 못 (*Nail*): [Horizontal / Vertical]
9. 밀 (*Wheat*): [Horizontal / Vertical]
10. 발 (*Foot*): [Horizontal / Vertical]

Exercise 4. Determine if the following words have final consonants:

1. 사람 (*Human*): [Yes / No]
2. 바다 (*Ocean*): [Yes / No]
3. 책 (*Book*): [Yes / No]
4. 추위 (*Cold*): [Yes / No]
5. 책상 (*Desk*): [Yes / No]
6. 위기 (*Crisis*): [Yes / No]
7. 바람 (*Wind*): [Yes / No]
8. 문 (*Door*): [Yes / No]
9. 바닥 (*Floor*): [Yes / No]
10. 책임 (*Responsibility*): [Yes / No]

Exercise 5. Explain how the following words are organized:

Example: 흙 (*Soil*) = Consonant + Horizontal vowel + (Final consonant + Final consonant)

1. 강 (*River*) = _____
2. 달 (*Moon*) = _____
3. 재 (*Ash*) = _____
4. 병 (*Disease/Bottle*) = _____
5. 운 (*Luck*) = _____
6. 닭 (*Chicken*) = _____
7. 약 (*Medicine*) = _____
8. 배 (*Pear/Belly/Ship*) = _____
9. 해 (*Sun*) = _____
10. 삶 (*Life*) = _____

B. Final Consonants and the Korean Alphabet

Exercise 6. Fill in the blanks to complete the following table:

Plain	가	다	바	사	아	자
Aspirated	1._____	타	3._____	–	5._____	차
Tensed	까	2._____	빠	4._____	–	6._____

Exercise 7. Determine if the following vowels are Complex / Compound:

1. ㅐ : [Complex / Compound]
2. ㅘ : [Complex / Compound]
3. ㅔ : [Complex / Compound]
4. ㅚ : [Complex / Compound]
5. ㅒ : [Complex / Compound]
6. ㅙ : [Complex / Compound]
7. ㅝ : [Complex / Compound]
8. ㅞ : [Complex / Compound]
9. ㅖ : [Complex / Compound]
10. ㅢ : [Complex / Compound]

Exercise 8. Make compound vowels using the following vowels:

1. ㅗ + ㅏ = _____
2. ㅗ + ㅣ = _____
3. ㅗ + ㅐ = _____
4. ㅜ + ㅓ = _____
5. ㅜ + ㅔ = _____
6. ㅜ + ㅣ = _____
7. ＋ ㅣ = _____

Exercise 9. Determine if the following statement are True / False:

1. The consonant "ㄴ" does not have an aspirated counterpart. [True / False]
2. The Consonant "ㅇ" does not have a tensed counterpart. [True / False]
3. The consonant "ㄴ" has a tensed counterpart. [True / False]
4. The consonant "ㄹ" does not have an aspirated counterpart. [True / False]
5. The consonant "ㅁ" has an aspirated counterpart. [True / False]
6. The consonant "ㅅ" does not have an aspirated counterpart. [True / False]
7. The consonant "ㄹ" has a tensed counterpart. [True / False]
8. The consonant "ㅁ" does not have a tensed counterpart. [True / False]
9. The consonant "ㅇ" does not have an aspirated counterpart. [True / False]
10. The consonant "ㅅ" has a tensed counterpart. [True / False]

Exercise 10. Determine if the descriptions of the following syllable blocks are Correct / Incorrect:

1. 개 (*Dog*) = Consonant + Vowel [Correct / Incorrect]
2. 귤 (*Tangerine*) = Consonant + Vowel + Final consonant [Correct / Incorrect]
3. 껌 (*Chewing gum*) = Consonant + Vowel [Correct / Incorrect]
4. 꿈 (*Dream*) = Consonant + Vowel + Final Consonant [Correct / Incorrect]
5. 꾀 (*Trick*) = Consonant + Vowel + Final Consonant [Correct / Incorrect]
6. 꿀 (*Honey*) = Consonant + Vowel + Final Consonant [Correct / Incorrect]
7. 끝 (*End*) = Consonant + Vertical vowel + Final Consonant [Correct / Incorrect]
8. 밤 (*Night*) = Consonant + Vowel + Final Consonant [Correct / Incorrect]
9. 낮 (*Afternoon*) = Consonant + Vertical vowel [Correct / Incorrect]
10. 눈 (*Eye/Snow*) = Consonant + Complex vowel + Final consonant [Correct / Incorrect]

ANSWERS:

Exercise 1

1. 각: 2 (ㄱ, ㄱ) / 2. 간: 2 (ㄱ, ㄴ) / 3. 금: 2 (ㄱ, ㅁ) / 4. 곰: 2 (ㄱ, ㅁ) / 5. 띠: 1 (ㄸ) / 6. 값: 3 (ㄱ, ㅂ, ㅅ) / 7. 넋: 3 (ㄴ, ㄱ, ㅅ) / 8. 반: 2 (ㅂ, ㄴ) / 9. 사: 1 (ㅅ) / 10. 탑: 2 (ㅌ, ㅂ)

Exercise 2

1. ㅓ: Basic / 2. ㅏ: Basic / 3. ㅖ: Complex / 4. ㅓ: Basic / 5. ㅓ: Basic / 6. ㅗ: Basic / 7. ㅡ: Basic / 8. ㅏ: Basic / 9. ㅖ: Complex / 10. ㅟ: Compound

Exercise 3

1. ㅓ: Vertical / 2. ㅗ: Horizontal / 3. ㅡ: Horizontal / 4. ㅏ: Vertical / 5. ㅡ: Horizontal / 6. ㅏ: Vertical / 7. ㅓ: Vertical / 8. ㅗ: Horizontal / 9. ㅣ: Vertical / 10. ㅏ: Vertical

Exercise 4

1. Yes (ㅁ) / 2. No / 3. Yes (ㄱ) / 4. No / 5. Yes (ㄱ, ㅇ) / 6. No / 7. Yes (ㅁ) / 8. Yes (ㄴ) / 9. Yes (ㄱ) / 10. Yes (ㄱ, ㅁ)

Exercise 5

1. 강 = Consonant + Vertical vowel + Final consonant / 2. 달 = Consonant + Vertical vowel + Final consonant / 3. 재 = Consonant + Compound vowel / 4. 병 = Consonant + Vertical vowel + Final consonant / 5. 운 = Consonant + Horizontal vowel + Final consonant / 6. 닭 = Consonant + Vertical vowel + (Final consonant + Final consonant) / 7. 약 = Consonant + Vertical vowel + Final consonant / 8. 배 = Consonant + Compound vowel / 9. 해 = Consonant + compound vowel / 10. 삶 = Consonant + Vertical vowel + (Final consonant + Final consonant

Exercise 6

1. 카 / 2. 따 / 3. 파 / 4. 싸 / 5. 하 / 6. 짜

Exercise 7

1. ㅐ: Complex / 2. ㅘ: Compound / 3. ㅔ: Complex / 4. ㅚ: Compound / 5. ㅒ: Complex / 6. ㅙ: Compound / 7. ㅝ: Compound / 8. ㅞ: Compound / 9. ㅖ: Complex / 10. ㅢ: Compound

Exercise 8

1. ᅪ / 2. ᅬ / 3. ᅫ / 4. ᅯ / 5. ᅰ / 6. ᅱ / 7. ᅴ

Exercise 9

1. True / 2. True / 3. False: The consonant "ㄴ" does not have a tensed counterpart. / 4. True / 5. False: The consonant "ㅁ" does not have an aspirated counterpart. / 6. True / 7. False: The consonant "ㄹ" does not have a tensed counterpart. / 8. True / 9. False: The aspirated counterpart of the consonant "ㅇ" is the consonant "ㅎ." / 10. True

Exercise 10

1. True / 2. True / 3. False: 껌 = Consonant + Vowel + Final consonant / 4. True / 5. False: 꾀: Consonant + Vowel / 6. True / 7. False: 끝: Consonant + Horizontal vowel + Final consonant / 8. True / 9. False: 낯 = Consonant + Vertical vowel + Final consonant / 10. False: 눈 = Consonant + Horizontal vowel + Final consonant

QUICK RECAP

In this lesson, we talked about syllable blocks and the final consonant. The final consonant (called "받침") is added to the bottom of the syllable block for syllables ending with a consonant.

This brings us to the end of the Korean alphabet series, and you have been introduced to every type of syllable block and shown examples of each. You should now have a better understanding of how the Korean consonants and vowels are combined to form various syllables.

The additional vocabulary given above, the syllable block chart below, as well as the words from lesson 2, should be enough to keep you busy until the next lesson. Be sure to also practice reading and writing the entire Hangul by putting the consonants and vowels together in different combinations. Happy practicing!

	Syllable Block Types	Examples
1	Consonant + Vertical Vowel	가, 나, 려, 더, 미
2	Consonant + Horizontal Vowel	고, 모, 누, 유, 스
3	Consonant + Compound Vowel	애, 세, 왜, 과, 휘
4	Consonant + Vertical Vowel + Final Consonant	안, 녕, 합, 같, 멋
5	Consonant + Horizontal Vowel + Final Consonant	물, 옷, 눈, 국, 솜
6	Consonant + Compound Vowel + Final Consonant	괜, 흰, 뭘
7	Consonant + Vertical Vowel + (Final Consonant + Final Consonant)	많, 덟, 있, 없, 찮
8	Consonant + Horizontal Vowel + (Final Consonant + Final Consonant)	흙, 꿇, 곪
9	Consonant + Compound Vowel + (Final Consonant + Final Consonant)	**Not used**

LESSON 4: KOREAN PARTICLES – TOPIC MARKER AND SUBJECT MARKER EXPLAINED

One of the most confusing aspects of Korean grammar for beginners is learning the difference between 은/는 and 이/가 and struggling to figure out which one to use in any given sentence. This is one of the most difficult concepts to master (and to explain) in beginning Korean, but we hope that by the end of this lesson you'll have a much better grasp of it!

Particles (markers) 은/는 and 이/가 are attached to the topic or the subject of a sentence

은/는 is often referred to as the *topic marker*, and 이/가 the *subject marker*. However, the topic and the subject are not always easily determined in a sentence. A sentence can have both a topic and a subject; but in many cases, the topic can also be the subject and vice versa. Students tend to get even more confused by using the terms *topic marker* and *subject marker*.

Rather than focusing on the terminology, it's better to focus on the *function* of the particles and explain the differences. Please feel free to use the terms *topic marker* and *subject marker* if doing so helps your learning. Ultimately, understanding what each particle *does* is more important than trying to correctly label the particles.

Before we go on, we should point out that 은 and 는 are the same particle, except that 은 follows a consonant and 는 follows a vowel. Similarly, 이 and 가 are the same particle. 이 follows a consonant and 가 follows a vowel.

Rule #1: When deciding between Korean particles 은/는 vs. 이/가, ask yourself one question:

Where in the sentence is the **key message** you want to convey — the **subject** or the **predicate**?

The subject is what the sentence is about, and the predicate gives information about the subject.

Subject + Predicate	Subject + Predicate
If the subject has the key message, use **이/가**	If the predicate has the key message, use 은/는

Listen to Track 19

Let's look at some examples by comparing the differences in meaning between 은/는 and 이/가 in otherwise identical sentences.

- 이 사람**은** 제이슨이에요. *(This person is **Jason**.)*
  이 사람**이** 제이슨이에요. ***(This person is** Jason) (This is Jason, not someone else.)*

- 제이슨**은** 의사예요. *(Jason is **a doctor**.) (Doctor is his profession.)*
  제이슨**이** 의사예요. ***(Jason** is the doctor.) (Not someone else.)*

- 린다**는** 선생님이에요. *(Linda is **a teacher**.) (Teacher is her profession.)*
  린다**가** 선생님이에요. ***(Linda** is the teacher.) (Not someone else.)*

Notice that in English, using the words "a" or "the" changes the meaning of the message. In Korean sentences, the particles serve the same purpose.

Let's look at some more examples. In order to know what part of the sentence is more important, think about what the question is that these statements are answering. Then determine if the answer is in the subject or the predicate of the sentence.

Listen to Track 20

(Question: Who is the President of the U.S.?)

- 미국 대통령**은** 조 바이든이에요. *(The president of the U.S. is **Joe Biden**.)*
- 조 바이든**이** 미국 대통령이에요. ***(Joe Biden** is the president of the U.S.)*

In answering the question *"Who is the President of the U.S.?"*

➢ 은 is used with the first sentence because the answer is in the predicate of the sentence.

➢ 이 is used in the second sentence because the answer is in the subject of the sentence.

Listen to Track 21

(Question: Who is Joe Biden?)

- 조 바이든**은 미국 대통령**이에요. *(Joe Biden is **the president of the U.S.**)*

In answering the question *"Who is Joe Biden?"*

➢ 은 is used with the subject because the answer is in the predicate of the sentence.

Below are more examples:

Listen to Track 22

- **우리 강아지가** 제 숙제를 먹었어요. ***(Our puppy** ate my homework.)*
  (This statement explains what happened to the homework, and "our puppy" is the more important information.)

- 우리 강아지**는 장난감을 좋아해요.** *(Our puppy **likes toys.**)*
  (This statement gives information about the puppy, so the predicate "likes toys" is more important.)

Still confused? Here's an even simpler way to think about 은/는 vs. 이/가:

> - **이/가** implies "I just stated the important information before this marker."
> - **은/는** implies "the important information is still to come after this marker."

Rule #2: Use the Korean particle 은/는 to compare or contrast with another statement

---

Although the above Rule #1 applies in general, there are exceptions. One exception would be to compare and/or contrast statements.

Here are some examples:

Listen to Track 23

Example 1:

Q: Do you know where I can buy some groceries?

A:

- **슈퍼가** 여기에서 멀어요. *(The supermarket is far from here.)*
- 시장**은** 가까워요. *(The outdoor market is close by.)*

Example 1 is in response to someone needing to buy some groceries. The two statements indicate that the supermarket is far away but the outdoor market is close by. The subject of the second sentence (시장) has the particle 은, because the distance to the outdoor market is compared with the first sentence.

If the question was "Where is the supermarket?", then the first sentence would have been "슈퍼는 **여기에서 멀어요**," in line with Rule #1 (subject-predicate) explained above.

Listen to Track 24

Example 2:

Q: What subjects are you struggling with?

A:

- **영어가** 어려워요. *(English is difficult.)*
- 수학은 쉬워요. *(Math is easy.)*

The above two statements compare English and math in response to the question. The subject of the second sentence (수학) has the particle 은, because the person is saying math is easy in comparison to English.

Again, if the question was "How are you doing in English?", then the first sentence would have been "영어는 **어려워요**."

Listen to Track 25

Example 3:

- **그 사람의 옷차림이** 재미있어요. *(That person's clothing style is fun.)*
- 모자는 빨간색이에요. *(The hat is red.)*
- 코트는 보라색이에요. *(The coat is purple.)*
- 그리고 바지는 노란색이에요. *(And the pants are yellow.)*

After the initial statement, the next three sentences compare the different colors of the different pieces of clothing the person is wearing. 은/는 is used in each of those sentences because they are in contrast with each other.

Rule #3: When a Korean sentence contains both topic and subject - use 은/는 with the topic and 이/가 with the subject

A unique feature in Korean grammar is the "**double subject**." Subject A indicates the "topic" of the sentence (using 은/은 as the topic marker), while subject B performs the normal function of subject (using 이/가 as the subject marker.) It can neither be clearly explained by Korean linguists, nor is it clearly translatable. Please note that Korean sometimes uses double subjects to indicate adverbs, objects, or other sentence elements.

Here are some examples of this:

Listen To Track 26

- 저는 머리가 아파요. *(As for me, my head hurts.)*
- 올해는 태풍이 너무 많았어요. *(As for this year, there were too many hurricanes.)*
- 오늘은 날씨가 좋아요. *(As for today, the weather is nice.)*

This is where the terms "topic marker" and "subject marker" make sense. In each of the above sentences, the first part is the topic, so 은/는 follows the topic. The second part in each sentence is the actual subject noun and is followed by 이/가.

Exception to Rule #3:

There is an exception to the above rule, wherein the sentence implies that the stated information contrasts with all other possible options. The implied information is shown in parentheses.

Listen To Track 27

- 제가 피부는 안 좋아요.

  Meaning: *As for me, my complexion is bad (but everything else about me is good).*

- 그 여자가 성격은 좋아요.

  Meaning: *As for that woman, she has a good personality (but no other good qualities).*

- 이 식당이 고기 종류는 맛이

  Meaning: *As for this restaurant, the meat dishes are good (but not other dishes)*

Because the subject of each statement is using 은/는 (for contrast), the topic has to use 이/가. In most cases, if 은/는 follows the topic, 이/가 follows the subject; and if 이/가 follows the topic, 은/는 follows the subject.

Let's look at the same examples with the particles switched. The sentences below are similar to the examples first given for Rule #3. You should notice that when written this way, there are no implied meanings.

Listen To Track 28

- 저는 피부**가** 안 좋아요. *(As for me, my complexion is bad.)*
- 그 여자**는** 성격**이** 좋아요. *(As for that woman, she has a good personality.)*
- 이 식당**은** 고기 종류**가** 맛이 있어요. *(As for this restaurant, the meat dishes are good.)*

These sentences simply contain the topic and one piece of information about the topic. There is no implied information.

> ***Note:** There are some instances when 이/가 is used for both the topic and the subject, but you will *almost never* see 은/는 used back to back for the topic and the subject.

TIME TO PRACTICE!

Korean Particles – Topic Marker and Subject Marker Explained

Exercise 1. Choose the right particle in the following sentences:

1. 빌딩 [이 / 가] 높아요. *(The building is tall.)*
2. 사람 [이 / 가] 많아요. *(There are many people.)*
3. 다리 [이 / 가] 아파요. *(My legs hurt.)*
4. 가격 [이 / 가] 비싸요. *(It is expensive.)*
5. 하늘 [이 / 가] 매우 맑아요. *(The sky is very clear.)*
6. 셔츠 [이 / 가] 너무 작아요. *(The shirt is too small.)*
7. 사슴 [이 / 가] 도망갔어요. *(The deer ran away.)*
8. 비행기 [이 / 가] 도착했어요. *(The airplane has arrived.)*
9. 어떤 색 [이 / 가] 좋아요? *(Which color do you like?)*
10. 도둑 [이 / 가] 체포됐어요. *(The thief is under arrest.)*

Exercise 2. Choose the right particle in the following sentences:

1. 테사 [은 / 는] 20살이에요. *(Tessa is 20 years old.)*
2. 나 [은 / 는] 영국인이에요. *(I am British.)*
3. 내 누나 [은 / 는] 대학생이에요. *(My sister is a college student.)*
4. 김치 [은 / 는] 한국 음식이에요. *(Kimchi is a Korean food.)*
5. 서울 [은 / 는] 한국의 수도에요. *(Seoul is the capital city of Korea.)*
6. 내 어머니 [은 / 는] 선생님이에요. *(My mother is a teacher.)*
7. 오늘 [은 / 는] 날씨가 맑아요. *(It is sunny today.)*
8. 용암 [은 / 는] 매우 뜨거워요. *(Lava is very hot.)*
9. 제 전공 [은 / 는] 컴퓨터 공학이에요. *(My major is computer science.)*
10. 맥킨지 [은 / 는] 작가가 되고 싶어요. *(Mackenzie wants to be a writer.)*

Exercise 3. Determine if the following sentences are Correct / Incorrect:

1. 나은 네가 좋다. [Correct / Incorrect] *(I like you.)*
2. 내 동생은 똑똑하다. [Correct / Incorrect] *(My brother is smart.)*
3. 고래는 크다. [Correct / Incorrect] *(Whales are big.)*
4. 천문학자이 또 다른 블랙홀을 발견했다. [Correct / Incorrect] *(The astronomer found another black hole.)*
5. 너는 어떤 장르의 영화를 좋아하니? [Correct / Incorrect] *(What kind of movies do you like?)*

6. 과거에 후추는 사치품이었다. [Correct / Incorrect] (*Pepper was a luxury in the past.*)
7. 데이빗는 한국어를 공부하는 중이다. [Correct / Incorrect] (*David is studying Korean.*)
8. 내 이름는 민수다. [Correct / Incorrect] (*My name is Minsu.*)
9. 나는 독서를 좋아한다. [Correct / Incorrect] (*I like reading books.*)
10. 경제가 악화되고 있다. [Correct / Incorrect] (*The economy is deteriorating.*)

Exercise 4. Determine if the key messages are in the Subject / Predicate in the sentences:

1. 이 사람은 미셸이에요. [Subject / Predicate] (*This person is Michelle.*)
2. 이 사람이 미셸이에요. [Subject / Predicate] (*This person is Michelle.*)
3. 제임스는 컴퓨터 프로그래머예요. [Subject / Predicate] (*James is a computer programmer.*)
4. 제임스가 컴퓨터 프로그래머예요. [Subject / Predicate] (*James is the computer programmer.*)
5. 사과는 맛있어요. [Subject / Predicate] (*Apples are delicious.*)
6. 사과가 맛있어요. [Subject / Predicate] (*This apple is delicious.*)
7. 비행기는 빨라요. [Subject / Predicate] (*Airplanes are fast.*)
8. 자동차가 빨라요. [Subject / Predicate] (*The car is fast.*)
9. 고양이는 귀여워요. [Subject / Predicate] (*Cats are cute.*)
10. 강아지가 귀여워요. [Subject / Predicate] (*The puppy is cute.*)

Exercise 5. Determine if the underlined particles indicate Topic / Subject:

1. **나는** 머리가 아프다. [Topic / Subject]
   (I have a headache.) (As for me, my head hurts.)
2. 올해는 **날씨가** 너무 덥다. [Topic / Subject]
   (It is too hot this year.) (As for this year, the weather is hot.)
3. **오늘은** 날씨가 좋다. [Topic / Subject]
   (The weather is nice today.) (As for today, the weather is nice.)
4. **내일은** 비가 올 예정이다. [Topic / Subject]
   (It will rain tomorrow.) (As for tomorrow, the rain will come.)
5. 나는 **네가** 좋다. [Topic / Subject]
   (I like you.) (As for me, you are good.)
6. 나는 **삼겹살이** 좋다. [Topic / Subject]
   (I like Korean BBQ.) (As for me, Korean BBQ is good.)
7. **나는** IQ가 높다. [Topic / Subject]
   (I have a high IQ.) (As for me, IQ is high.)

8. **오늘은** 할 일이 없다. [Topic / Subject]

   (I have nothing to do today.) (As for today, there is nothing to do.)

9. 올해는 짧은 **머리가** 유행이다. [Topic / Subject]

   (Short hair is in fashion this year.) (As for this year, short hair is popular.)

10. **나는** 해야 할 일이 많다. [Topic / Subject]

   (I have many things to do.) (As for me, there are many things to do.)

ANSWERS:

Exercise 1

1. 이 / 2. 이 / 3.가 / 4. 이 / 5. 이 / 6. 가 / 7. 이 / 8. 가 / 9. 이 / 10. 이

Exercise 2

1. 는 / 2. 는 / 3. 는 / 4. 는 / 5. 은 / 6. 는 / 7. 은 / 8. 은 / 9. 은 / 10. 는

Exercise 3

1. Incorrect: 나은 -> 나는 / 2. Correct / 3. Correct / 4. Incorrect: 천문학자이 -> 천문학자가 / 5. Correct / 6. Correct / 7. Incorrect: 데이빗는 -> 데이빗은 / 8. Incorrect: 이름는 -> 이름은 / 9. Correct / 10. Correct

Exercise 4

1. Predicate: the particle "은" indicates that the predicate has the key message.
2. Subject: the particle "이" indicates that the subject has the key message.
3. Predicate: the particle "는" indicates that the predicate has the key message.
4. Subject: the particle "가" indicates that the subject has the key message.
5. Predicate: the particle "는" indicates that the predicate has the key message.
6. Subject: the particle "가" indicates that the subject has the key message.
7. Predicate: the particle "는" indicates that the predicate has the key message.
8. Subject: the particle "가" indicates that the subject has the key message.
9. Predicate: the particle "는" indicates that the predicate has the key message.
10. Subject: the particle "가" indicates that the subject has the key message.

Exercise 5

1. Topic (As for me) / 2. Subject / 3. Topic (As for today) / 4. Topic (As for tomorrow) / 5. Subject / 6. Subject / 7. Topic (As for me) / 8. Topic (As for today) / 9. Subject / 10. Topic (As for me)

QUICK RECAP

We hope you now have a better understanding of the Korean particles 은/는 vs. 이/가. The principle surrounding which particle to use in any given sentence is one of the most difficult things to comprehend, and only time and experience with using the language will help you master it.

In this lesson, we have outlined three rules to keep in mind and provided various examples of how to differentiate between the two. Just remember that almost everyone struggles with this. As you continue reading and studying Korean on your own, try to make a note of which particles are used in each sentence. You will eventually get it!

LESSON 5: HOW TO INTRODUCE YOURSELF IN KOREAN

In this lesson, we will learn about basic Korean grammar to use when you introduce yourself to others. After this lesson, you will be able to talk about your name, age, family members, hobbies, and other information to introduce yourself. Let's see how we can introduce ourselves in Korean.

저는 -이에요/예요 (I am OOO)

Listen to Track 29

"저는 –이에요" follows the "subject + subject complement" structure.

Note: Korean follows the "**subject + object + verb**" structure while English has the "**subject + verb + object**" structure.

Depending the last letter of the complement, it will either be followed by the ending "-이에요" or "-예요." If the last letter is a consonant, it will be followed by "-이에요." However, if the last letter is a vowel it will be followed by "-예요."

Listen to Track 30

저는	OOO	-이에요 or -예요
Subject	**Subject Complement** (Noun)	**Ending** Indicating Complement
I	name / age (-살) / job	am (equivalent translation)
I am (name / age / job).		

The Korean ending "-이에요/-예요" works the same way as the English verb "to be" does. While the English verb "be" indicates that the *following* noun or adjective is a subject complement, the ending "-이에요/-예요" indicates that the noun *preceding* it is a complement, due to the different sentence structure that Korean follows.

> **Note:** *While subjects and verbs are essential in English sentences, Korean sentences omit or do not require subjects or verbs in many cases. Thus, it is important to remember that there is no verb in this "저는 – 이에요" sentence.*

How to Use "저는 –이에요 / 예요"

Listen to Track 31

Although the grammar in "저는 –이에요" seems complicated, the way to use it is simple. You can just put a noun to describe yourself before the ending "-이에요." Remember that "-이에요" is used when the noun ends with a consonant, and "-예요" is used when the noun ends with a vowel.

To tell someone your name

Listen to Track 32

- 저는 제임스**예요**. *(I am James.)*
  As the noun "제임스" ends with a vowel, "-예요" is used. Please remember even though "-예요" means the English verb "be" in the translation, it is not a verb but rather an ending indicating the complement.

- 저는 레이첼**이에요**. *(I am Rachel.)*
  As the noun "레이첼" ends with a consonant, "-이에요" is used.

To tell someone your age

Listen to Track 33

- 저는 25살**이에요**. **(Correct)** *(I am 25 years old.)*
  The word "살" means "years old" when it is connected to numbers.

- 살이에요. **(Incorrect)**
  The word "살" is a bound noun (dependent noun). Dependent nouns cannot be used alone; they have meanings only when connected to other nouns.

To tell someone about your job (position)

Listen to Track 34

- 저는 사장**이에요.** **(Correct)** *(I am the CEO.)*
  You can tell someone about your position in your company.

- 저는 사진사**예요.** **(Correct)** *(I am a photographer.)*
  You can tell someone about your job.

- 저는 **병원이**에요. **(Incorrect)** *(I am **a clinic.**)*
  You cannot tell someone about your workplace with "-이에요." You will learn how to tell someone about your workplace in the following lesson.

저는 –이 / -가 있어요 (I have OOO)

Listen to Track 35

The structure of this sentence is "**subject A + subject B + ending.**" This is the "double subject" structure that we introduced in the last lesson! The word "있어요" has the meaning of the English verb "exist."

저는	OOO	-이 / -가	있어요
Subject A (just in the form)	**Subject B** (connected to adjective)	**Subject Marker** indicating subject B	**Verb**
저는	여동생	이	있어요
I ('as for me')	*sister*	*is*	*existing*
As for me, the sister is existing -> I have a sister.			

How to Use "저는 –이 / -가 있어요"

Listen to Track 36

To say you have a family member

The grammar in "저는 –이 / -가 있어요" is very difficult. Luckily, the way to use it is simple. You just put "-이" or "-가" after the noun. When the noun ends with a vowel you should use "-**가.**" When it ends with a consonant, you should use "-이."

- 저는 동생**이 있어요**. *(I **have** a younger sister or brother.)*
  The subject marker "-이" is used as the noun "동생" ends with a consonant.

- 저는 누나**가 있어요**. *(I **have** an older sister.)*
  The marker "-가" is used as the noun "누나" ends with a vowel.

저의 취미는 –이에요 (My hobby is OOO)

Listen to Track 37

The grammar in "저의 취미는 –이에요" follows the "**subject + subject complement**" structure. Please remember that Korean uses the ending to indicate subject complement as Korean does not have the verb "be."

저의	취미는	OOO	-이에요 / 예요
Modifier for Subject	**Subject**	**Subject Complement**	**Ending** Indicating Subject Complement
저의	취미는	춤추는 것	이에요
My	*hobby*	*dancing*	*is (in translation)*
My hobby is dancing.			

You can put the ending "-이에요" after activities. When the noun ends with a consonant, you should use "-이에요."

Listen to Track 38

How to Use "저의 취미는 –이에요"

To tell someone your hobby

- 저의 취미는 등산**이에요**. *(My hobby **is** climbing.)*
  As the noun "등산" ends with a consonant, "-이에요" is used.

- 저의 취미는 축구**예요**. *(My hobby **is** [playing] soccer.)*
  As the noun "축구" ends with a vowel, only "-예요" is used.

저는 –에서 살아요 (I live in OOO)

Finally, we are seeing a familiar structure! "저는 –에서 살아요" follows the "**subject + verb**" structure. It means "I live in [a place]" in English.

Listen to Track 39

저는	OOO	-에서	살아요
Subject	**Noun**	**Location Marker**	**Verb**
저는	서울	에서	살아요
I	*Seoul*	*in*	*to live*
I live in Seoul.			

Listen to Track 39

Listen to Track 39

How to Use "저는 –에서 살아요"

To tell someone where you live

- 저는 한국**에서 살아요.** *(I **live in** Korea.)*
- 저는 서울**에서 살아요.** *(I **live in** Seoul.)*
- 저는 시골**에서 살아요.** *(I **live in** the countryside.)*

저는 –에서 일해요 (I am working for/at OOO)

Like the previous sentence, 저는 –에서 일해요" follows the "**subject + verb**" structure." It means, "I work for/at [place]" in English.

Listen to Track 40

저는	OOO	-에서	일해요
Subject	**Noun**	**Location Marker**	**Verb**
저는	학교	에서	일해요
I	*school*	*at*	*to work*
I work at the school.			

How to Use "저는 –에서 일해요"

To tell someone about your workplace

- 저는 병원**에서 일해요**. (*I **work at/for** the hospital.*)
- 저는 동물원**에서 일해요**. (*I **work at/for** the zoo.*)
- 저는 **의사**에서 일해요. **(Incorrect)** (*I **work at a doctor.***)

You cannot tell someone about your job position using "저는 –에서 일해요." You should say "저는 의사예요 (I am a doctor)" instead.

TIME TO PRACTICE!

How to Introduce Yourself in Korean

Exercise 1. Fill in the blanks to complete the following sentences:

1. 저는 수지 _____. *(My name is Suji.)*
2. 저는 21살 _____. *(I am 21 years old.)*
3. 저는 간호사 _____. *(I am a nurse.)*
4. 저는 무역 회사의 과장 _____. *(I am a section chief in an international trade company.)*
5. 저의 취미는 낚시 _____. *(My hobby is fishing.)*
6. 저는 제주도에서 _____. *(I live in Jeju Island.)*
7. 저는 남동생이 _____. *(I have a younger brother.)*
8. 저는 대학교에서 _____. *(I work at a college.)*
9. 저의 _____는 축구에요. *(My hobby is playing soccer.)*
10. 저는 부산에서 _____. *(I live in Busan.)*

Exercise 2. Determine if the following sentences are Correct / Incorrect:

1. 저는 병원이에요. *(I work at a hospital.)* _____
2. 저는 25살이에요. *(I am 25 years old.)* _____
3. 저는 학생에요. *(I am a student.)* _____
4. 저는 사장이에요. *(I am the CEO of a company.)* _____
5. 저는 여동생가 있어요. *(I have a younger sister.)* _____
6. 저는 누나가 있어요. *(I have an older sister.)* _____
7. 저의 취미는 등산에요. *(My hobby is climbing.)* _____
8. 저는 한국에서 살아요. *(I live in Korea.)* _____
9. 저는 의사에서 일해요. *(I am a doctor.)* _____
10. 저는 동물원에서 일해요. *(I work at a zoo.)* _____

Exercise 3. Choose the right word in the following sentences:

1. 저는 제임스 [**이에요** / **예요**]. *(My name is James.)* _____
2. 저는 레이첼 [**이에요** / **예요**]. *(I am Rachel.)* _____
3. 저의 취미는 게임 [**이에요** / **예요**]. *(My hobby is playing video games.)*
_____

4. 저는 형 [**이** / **가**] 있어요. *(I have an older brother.)* _____
5. 저는 할머니와 할아버지 [**이** / **가**] 있어요. *(I have a grandmother and grandfather.)* _____
6. 저는 여동생 [**이** / **가**] 있어요. *(I have a younger sister.)* _____
7. 저는 선생님 [**이에요** / **에요**]. *(I am a teacher.)* _____
8. 저는 병원에서 [**일해요** / **살아요**]. *(I work at a clinic.)* _____
9. 저는 미국에서 [**일해요** / **살아요**]. *(I live in the U.S.)* _____
10. 저는 프랑스에서 선생님으로 [**일해요** / **살아요**]. *(I work as a teacher in France.)* _____

Exercise 4. Determine if the following statements are True / False:

1. You have to use 살 when you tell some your age. _____
2. 살 is not a bound noun (dependent noun). _____
3. "-이에요" is connected to a noun. _____
4. "-이에요" indicates an object. _____
5. Using "-이에요," you can tell someone your age and job. _____
6. 살아요 means "to live" in English. _____
7. 일해요 is an adjective. _____
8. 취미 means "hobby" in English. _____
9. You can use only a noun or a pronoun before "-이에요." _____
10. There are two subjects in "저는 -이(가) 있어요." _____

Exercise 5. Fill in the blanks in the following explanations:

1. To tell someone your name: 저는 OOO _____.
2. To say you have a family member: 저는 OOO이(가) _____.
3. To tell someone your age: 저는 OO살 _____.
4. To tell someone your hobby: 저의 _____ 는 OOO이에요.
5. To tell someone about your job: 저는 OOO _____.
6. To tell someone where you live: 저는 OOO에서 _____.
7. To tell someone about your workplace: 저는 OOO에서 _____.

ANSWERS:

Exercise 1

1. 예요 / 2. 이예요 / 3. 에요 / 4. 이에요 / 5. 에요 / 6. 살아요 / 7. 있어요 / 8. 일해요 / 9. 취미 / 10. 살아요

Exercise 2

1. Incorrect (병원이에요 -> 병원에서 일해요) / 2. Correct / 3. Incorrect (학생에요 -> 학생이에요) / 4. Correct / 5. Incorrect (여동생가 -> 여동생이) / 6. Correct / 7. Incorrect (등산에요 -> 등산이에요) / 8. Correct / 9. Incorrect (의사에서 일해요 -> 의사에요) / 10. Correct

Exercise 3

1. 예요 / 2. 이예요 / 3. 이에요. / 4. 이 / 5. 가 / 6. 이 / 7. 이에요 / 8. 일해요 / 9. 살아요 / 10. 일해요

Exercise 4

1. True / 2. False (it is a bound noun) / 3. True / 4. False (it indicates complement) / 5. True / 6. True / 7. False (it is a verb) / 8. True / 9. True / 10. True

Exercise 5

1. 예요 / 2. 있어요 / 3. 이에요. / 4. 취미 / 5. 이에요 / 6. 살아요 / 7. 일해요

QUICK RECAP

Today, you learned about how to introduce yourself and related Korean grammar. Introducing yourself in Korean can be easy as you can just put nouns before endings. However, the grammar for the introduction can be tricky even though it is basic grammar. Let's review the grammar section. You did a good job today!

Listen to Track 41

I am (name / age / job).		
저는	Name	-이에요 / 예요
저는	Age + -살	-이에요
저는	Job / Position	-이에요 / 예요
I have (family member).			
저는	Family member	-이 / -가	있어요
My hobby is (activity).			
저의	취미는	Activity	-이에요 / 예요
I live in (place).			
저는	Nation / City / Place	-에서	살아요
I work at/for (workplace).			
저는	Workplace	-에서	일해요

LESSON 6: HOW TO SAY THIS, THAT, HERE AND THERE – 이것/저것/그것 & 여기/저기/거기

T he first thing you should be aware of regarding the words **"this,"** **"that,"** **"here,"** and **"there"** in Korean is that there are <u>two words</u> for "that" and also <u>two words</u> for "there."

In this lesson, we will go over the differences between the words and how they are used in sentences. We would also like to note that, starting from this lesson, we will no longer be using romanization for the examples we present! This is to further your reading ability and get you used to relying on memorization of the characters!

이것/저것/그것 (this/that/that)

In English, the word "that" is used to describe everything that does not qualify as "this." However, in the Korean language, there are three categories of such words:

Listen to Track 42

- 이것 This thing in front of me or in front of us
- 저것 That thing over there that we both can point to
- 그것 That thing in front of you or that thing that you have, or the thing that I/we are thinking of or referring to (and cannot point to).

Here are some images to give you some visual references:

This thing in front of us:

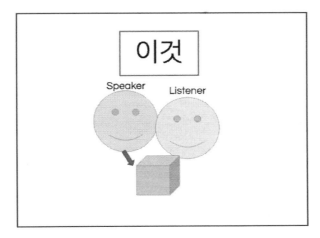

This thing in front of me:

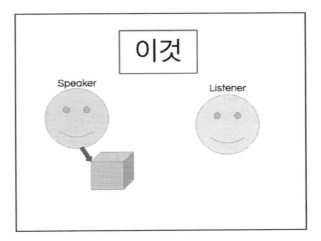

That thing over there that we can both point to:

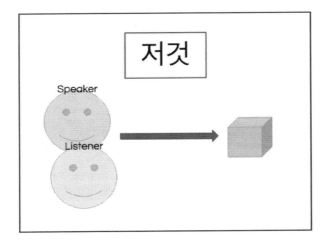

That thing that I am pointing to and also far from you:

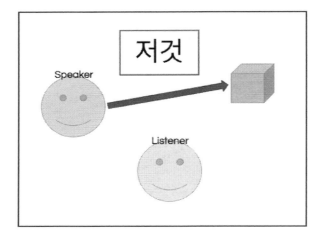

That thing in front of you, or that thing that you have:

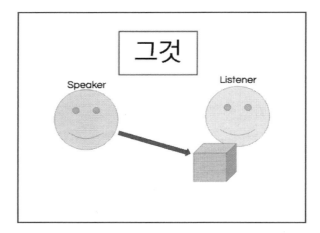

The thing that I/we are thinking of or referring to:

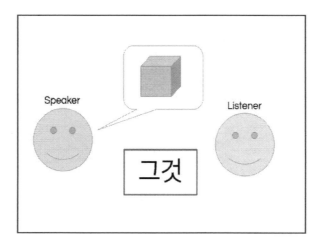

Did the images make the words more clear in your mind? We hope so!

Now let's talk about the structure of the words themselves. The first part of the words, **이, 저**, and **그**, are the actual parts that indicate *"this,"* *"that,"* and *"that."* The second part, **것**, is the word for *"thing."* Therefore, **이것** actually means *"this thing,"* **저것** means *"that thing (over there),"* and **그것** means *"that thing (that we are referring to)."*

However, the parts 이, 그, and 저 cannot stand on their own as independent words. They must be followed by a noun. They act as adjectives to describe the nouns that come after them.

Here are some examples:

Listen to Track 43

- 이 사람 *(This person)*
- 저 그림 *(That picture)*
- 그 식당 *(That restaurant)*

- 저 남자 *(That man)*
- 그 학생 *(That student)*
- 이 시간 *(This hour/time)*

One other thing we need to talk about in reference to the words 이것, 저것, and 그것 is the fact that in conversation, these words usually take on a more casual form as shown below:

Listen to Track 44

- 이것 → 이거
- 저것 → 저거
- 그것 → 그거

Dropping the final consonant makes it easier for conversation. But you should still remember to use the proper form for formal or business writing.

You should also be aware of the contractions when using the words with particles in sentences:

Listen to Track 45

Proper form	Conversational (casual)	Most commonly used(contraction)
이것은	이거는	이건
이것이	이게	이게
이것을	이거를	이걸

Let's look at some example sentences:

Listen to Track 46

Sentence	Pronunciation	Translation
이게 뭐예요?	[이게 모예요]	*What is this?*
저건 제가 만들었어요.	[저건 제가 만드러써요]	*I made that (thing over there).*
그건 어디에서 찾았어요?	[그건 어디에서 차자써요]	*Where did you find that (thing that you're holding)?*
저는 이걸 사고 싶어요.	[저는 이걸 사고 시퍼요]	*I want to buy this.*
그건 말이 안돼요.	[그건 마리 안돼요]	*That (what you're saying) makes no sense.*
이 영화가 아주 재밌어요.	[이 영화가 아주 재미써요]	*This movie is very fun/ interesting.*
저 그림이 더 멋있어요.	[저 그리미 더 머시써요]	*That picture (over there) is more stylish.*
그 사람이 회장이에요.	[그 사라미 회장이에요]	*That person (that you're referring to) is the CEO.*

Korean words 여기/저기/거기 (here/there/there)

Just as there are two different words for "that" in Korean, there are also two different words for "there." The concept is similar.

Listen to Track 47

- **여기** This place where we are or this place where I am
- **저기** That place over there that we both can point to
- **거기** That place where you are or the place that I/we are thinking of or referring to

It is important to note that the words **여기, 저기, 거기** are not their proper form. But they are the most commonly used words in conversation and casual writing.

You can see the proper form of the words below. They may make more logical sense to you:

Listen to Track 48

Word	Casual/Conversational	Proper
here	여기	이곳
there	저기	저곳
there	거기	그곳

You will notice that the words in the last column are very similar to **이것/저것/그것** *(this/that/that)*. The first part of the words, **이/저/그**, are the same; and the ending, **곳**, means "*place.*" That makes the translation of the words "this place," "that place (over there)," and "that place (that we're talking about)."

In formal settings and also in formal writing, you will often encounter the words **이곳, 저곳,** and **그곳**. In conversation, however, the words **여기, 저기,** and **거기** are almost always used.

One other thing to mention is that since these words indicate a location or place, the Korean particles **에** *(to, at)*, **에서/서** *(from)*, **까지** *(to)*, and **로** *(to, towards)* are often used with them.

Let's take a look at some example sentences:

Listen to Track 49

Sentence	Pronunciation	Translation
여기가 어디에요?	[여기가 어디에요]	*Where is here (where are we)?*
저기로 가면 큰 길이 나와요.	[저기로 가면 큰 기리 나와요]	*If you go toward there (that direction), you will see a main road.*
거기는 가지 마세요	[거기는 가지 마세요]	*Don't go there (the place you're referring to).*
저는 여기서 기다릴게요.	[저는 여기서 기다릴께요]	*I will wait here.*
여기에서 거기까지 몇 시간 걸려요?	[여기에서 거기까지 면 씨간 걸려요]	*How many hours will it take to go from here to there (the place we're talking about)?*

우리 그곳에서 만나요.	[우리 그고세서 만나요] (Also: 우리 거기서 만나요.)	*Let's meet at that place.*
여기는 제가 있을 곳이 아니에요.	[여기는 제가 이쓸 꼬시 아니에요]	*Here is not where I should be.*
오늘은 여기까지만 합시다.	[오느른 여기까지만 합씨다]	*Let's stop here today. (Literally translated, "Let's do only up to here.")*

Are you familiar with the popular YouTube channel "영국남자: Korean Englishman (https://www.youtube.com/user/koreanenglishman/featured)"? The channel creators Josh and Ollie make videos about Korea and its culture on a weekly basis for millions of followers.

The reason we mention the channel is because they end each of their videos with the phrase, "오늘은 여기까지!" The phrase literally translates as, *"Today is to here,"* and it means, *"Today, we stop here,"* or *"That is all for today."* If you haven't seen their videos yet, they are a lot of fun to watch.

TIME TO PRACTICE!

How to Say This, That, Here and There – 이것/저것/그것 & 여기/저기/거기

Exercise 1. Write down the words described in the explanations below:

1. The thing in front of the speaker, or both the speaker and the listener - _____

2. The thing over there that both the speaker and the listener can point to - _____

3. The thing in front of the listener, or that neither the speaker nor the listener can see - _____

4. The place where the speaker is, or both the speaker and the listener are - _____

5. The place over there that the both the speaker and the listener can point to - _____

6. The place that the speaker cannot see - _____

Exercise 2. Fill in the blanks with (여기 / 저기 / 거기) to complete the sentences:

1. _____ 에서 잠시만 기다려주세요. *(Wait here for a minute.)*
2. _____ 에서 만나자. *(Let's meet there.) [on the phone]*
3. _____ 가 좋은 레스토랑이야? *(Is the restaurant there good?) [on the phone]*
4. _____ 가 내 고향이다. *(Here is my hometown.)*
5. _____ 저 사람 보여? *(Do you see the person over there?)*
6. _____ 거스름돈입니다. *(Here is your change.)*
7. _____ 그 영화배우가 있다. *(That actress is over there.)*
8. _____ 에 가만히 있어. *(Stay there.) [on the phone]*
9. _____ 로 가자. *(Let's go over there.)*
10. _____ 는 왜 갔는데? *(Why did you go there?) [on the phone]*

Exercise 3. Fill in the blanks (이것 / 저것 / 그것) to complete the sentences:

1. _____ 이 네 휴대전화니? *(Is that your phone?) [to a friend holding her phone]*

2. _____ 은 뭐야? *(What is that?) [seeing a UFO in the sky]*

3. _____ 은 아무도 모르는 곳에 숨겨져 있어. *(That thing is hidden somewhere nobody knows.)*
4. _____ 은 한국 음식이야. *(This is Korean food.)*
5. _____ 이 무엇인지는 아무도 모른다. *(Nobody knows what that is.)* *[talking about myths]*
6. _____ 이 맛있어 보이네요. *(That looks delicious.)*
7. _____ 은 내 새로운 귀걸이야. *(This is my new earrings.)*
8. _____ 은 부적이야. *(This is a talisman.)*
9. _____ 은 최신형 자동차이다. *(That is the brand-new car.)*
10. _____ 은 오래 전에 사라졌다. *(That thing disappeared a long time ago.)* *[talking about news]*

Exercise 4. Choose the right word inside the brackets to complete the sentences:

1. [여기 / 이것] _____로 오세요. *(Come here.)*
2. [여기 / 이것] _____에 놓으세요. *(Put that here.)*
3. [여기 / 이것] _____좀 먹어보세요. *(Try this food.)*
4. [저기 / 저것] _____은 뭔가요? *(What is that?)*
5. [저기 / 저것] _____이 예쁘네요. *(That looks beautiful.)*
6. [저기 / 저것] _____로 가보죠. *(Let's go there.)*
7. [거기 / 그것] _____로 가려면 어떻게 해야해요? *(How can I get there?)*
8. [거기 / 그것] _____에 대해서는 잘 몰라요. *(I do not know much about that.)*
9. [거기 / 그것] _____은 비밀이에요. *(That is a secret.)*
10. [거기 / 그것] _____에서 만나요. *(Let's meet there.)*

Exercise 5. Determine if the following sentences are Correct / Incorrect:

1. "여기" means "here." _____
2. "저것" and "그것" have the same meaning. _____
3. You can use "저것" to indicate something that the listener can see. _____
4. 그것 can also indicate something that the listener possesses. _____
5. 이것 indicates something far from the speaker. _____
6. 저기 and 거기 have different meanings in Korean. _____
7. 이것 indicates something that the speaker can point to. _____
8. 저것 indicates something that the speaker cannot see. _____
9. 여기 indicates a place far from the speaker. _____
10. 거기 indicates the place where the speaker is. _____

ANSWERS:

Exercise 1

1. 이것 / 2. 저것 / 3. 그것 / 4. 여기 / 5. 저기 / 6. 거기

Exercise 2

1. 여기 / 2. 거기 / 3. 거기 / 4. 여기 / 5. 저기 / 6. 여기 / 7. 저기 / 8. 거기 / 9. 저기 / 10. 거기

Exercise 3

1. 그것 / 2. 저것 / 3. 그것 / 4. 이것 / 5. 그것 / 6. 저것 / 7. 이것 / 8. 이것 / 9. 저것 / 10. 그것

Exercise 4

1. 여기 / 2. 여기 / 3. 이것 / 4. 저것 / 5. 저것 / 6. 저기 / 7. 거기 / 8. 그것 / 9. 그것 / 10. 거기

Exercise 5

1. Correct / 2. Incorrect: "저것" and "그것" have different meanings while they both are translated as "that (thing)." / 3. Correct / 4. Correct / 5. Incorrect: "이것" indicates something close to the speaker. / 6. Correct / 7. Correct / 8. Incorrect: "저것" indicates something that the speaker can point to. / 9. Incorrect: "여기" indicates the place where the speaker is. / 10. Incorrect: "거기" indicates the place where the listener is, or where the speaker can refer to.

QUICK RECAP

If you previously had any confusion about the words 이것 (이거), 저것 (저거), 그것 (그거), and 여기, 저기, 거기, we hope you no longer do after this lesson! With a little bit of practice, you will be able to distinguish between them with ease.

In this lesson, we began with the proper form, 이것/저것/그것 (this/that/that), in order to demonstrate the logical structure of the words. With the words 여기/저기/거기 (here/there/there), we started with the conversational form and then introduced the proper/formal version.

Particularly with these words, you should learn to recognize both the conversational and proper forms and also be able to use them interchangeably. Always keep in mind that you are likely to encounter all forms of the words depending on what you are reading or listening to!

LESSON 7: A BEGINNER'S GUIDE TO KOREAN NUMBERS

D id you know that there are two different number systems used in Korea? One is called the **native number system**, and the other is called the **Sino-Korean number system**. We'll learn about them here.

Interesting fact:	*Sino-Korean refers to words and numbers that originated from or were influenced by Chinese. About 60 percent of Korean vocabulary has Chinese roots and can be written in Chinese characters called 한자 (han-ja).*

Korean Native Numbers 1 to 99

Native numbers are the original Korean number system. These numbers are used for counting, for age, and for the hour portion of time.

Have you ever taken a Korean martial arts class? If you have, you might recognize the native numbers 1 to 10, or at least 1 to 8. In many martial arts schools, the instructors often use Korean numbers when counting the movements.

Let's look at the numbers 1 to 100:

Listen to Track 50

1	하나		10	열
2	둘		20	스물
3	셋		30	서른
4	넷		40	마흔
5	다섯		50	쉰

6	여섯		60	예순
7	일곱		70	일흔
8	여덟		80	여든
9	아홉		90	아흔
10	열			

Note that zero does not exist in native Korean numbers, since you cannot count something that does not exist. In addition, the native numbers only go up to 99. Beyond that, Sino-Korean numbers are used.

Just add the numbers 1 to 9 to the number 10 to get the numbers 11 to 19:

Listen to Track 51

- 11 = 열(10) + 하나(1) = 열하나
- 12 = 열(10) + 둘(2) = 열둘
- 13 = 열(10) + 셋(3) = 열셋

And so on.

Listen to Track 52

The numbers 21 to 99 work in the same way:

- 21 = 스물(20) + 하나(1) = 스물 하나
- 35 = 서른(30) + 다섯(5) = 서른 다섯
- 99 = 아흔(90) + 아홉(9) = 아흔 아홉

Sino-Korean Numbers 1 to 100

Sino-Korean numbers are, in some ways, easier to learn. As shown below, 20 to 90 use the same words for 2 to 9 combined with the word for 10.

Listen to Track 53

0	공 / 영		10	십
1	일		20	이십
2	이		30	삼십
3	삼		40	사십

4	사		50	오십
5	오		60	육십
6	육		70	칠십
7	칠		80	팔십
8	팔		90	구십
9	구		100	백
10	십			

Similar to the native numbers, once you memorize the numbers 1 to 10, the rest of the numbers are very logical:

Listen to Track 54

- 11 = 십(10) + 일(1) = 십일
- 23 = 이십(20) + 삼(3) = 이십삼
- 45 = 사십(40) + 오(5) = 사십오

And so on...

Following this pattern, you can read any number up to 100 in Korean!

Sino-Korean Numbers 100 and Up

As we have mentioned before, native numbers only go up to 100, but there is no limit to the Sino-Korean numbers. Let's look at the Sino-Korean numbers beyond 100:

Listen to Track 55

100	백
1,000	천
10,000	만
100,000	십만
1,000,000	백만
10,000,000	천만
100,000,000	억

Below are some examples of random Sino-Korean numbers.

Listen to Track 56

2,020	이천 이십
133	백 삼십 삼
2,351	이천 삼백 오십 일
75,954	칠만 오천 구백 오십사
500,000,000	오억

Keep in mind that you would never spell out the Sino-Korean numbers in Hangul. The above tables only show how to *read* them. The numbers are written in the numeric form.

Which Korean Number System to use? Native or Sino-Korean?

Koreans use both number systems on a regular basis. Each number system is used in different situations and for different purposes:

Native Numbers	Sino-Korean Numbers
For counting up to 99, age, time (hour)	For math, dates, addresses, phone numbers, money, measurements, time (minutes)

Let's look at some examples of native numbers in a sentence:

• **Native Numbers**

Listen to Track 57

저는 **18**살이에요. [저는 **열려덜**살 이에요]	*I am **18** years old.*
우리 집에 고양이 **일곱** 마리가 있어요.	*There are **seven** cats at our house.*
오늘 연습을 **서른** 번도 더 했어요.	*I practiced more than **30** times today.*

Notice that the age 18 is written in the numeric form. You will often see that in writing, but you should still read it as a native number 열여덟.

Now let's look at some example sentences with Sino-Korean numbers. Sino-Korean numbers are usually written in the numeric form. The pronunciations are in brackets.

- **Sino-Korean Numbers**

Listen to Track 58

2 더하기 4는 6 이에요. [**이** 더하기 **사**는 **육**이에요]	*2 plus 4 is 6.*
우리 집은 34호예요. [우리 집은 **삼십사 호예요**]	*Our home is number 34.*
제 전화번호는 010-2345-6789 이에요. [제 전화번호는 **공일공-이삼사오-** **육칠팔구** 이에요]	*My phone number is 010-2345-6789*
가격은 5불 50센트예요. [가격은 **오불 오십** 센트예요]	*The price is 5 dollars and 50 cents.*

When it comes to telling time, both the native and Sino-Korean numbers are used. Native numbers are used for the hour and Sino-Korean numbers are used for the minutes.

Listen to Track 59

5:30	다섯 시 삼십 분
12:15	열두 시 십오 분
9:00	아홉 시

We're assuming that you are thoroughly confused by now. It will take some practice to get used to using two different number systems for telling time.

It may be easier for you to comprehend the concept if you look at the time in a different way:

- Think of 5:30 as "the fifth hour and 30 minutes"
- Think of 12:15 as "the twelfth hour and 15 minutes"
- And think of 9:00 as "the ninth hour"

If you look at it that way, it does actually make sense, right?

Counters Used with Numbers

When a number is used in a sentence to indicate a quantity of things or people, a particle must accompany the number. These particles are often referred to as "counters." Counters are used with both native and Sino-Korean numbers.

In English sentences, we simply use the number as the adjective for the item or person that we're describing, such as ten cats, two apples, five men, etc. In a Korean sentence, you need to state the noun first and then add the number after the noun. The counter then comes after the number.

You can think of the counters as words to describe what is being counted. The Korean language has numerous counters for every type of noun. It will be almost impossible for you to learn all the counters at once, because there are so many. Just take one at a time as they come up and add them to your vocabulary.

Here are some common Korean counters to start you off (but not a full list):

Listen to Track 60

Native number counters
(up to a quantity of 99, use Sino-Korean numbers with the same counters)

마리	Animals: 고양이 **세 마리** (three cats), 개 **한 마리** (one dog)
명	People (general): 남자 **두 명** (two men)
분	People (formal): 손님 **두 분** (two guests)
개	All things that do not have their own designated counter: 사과 **한 개** (one apple), 과자 **두 개** (two cookies), 모자 **세 개** (three hats)
번	Number of times: 다시 **한번** (one more time), **열 번** (ten times), **두 세 번** (two or three times)
시	The hour portion of time: **한시** (one o'clock), **두시** (two o'clock), **세시** (three o'clock)
시간	Duration of time: **한 시간** (one hour), **열두 시간** (12 hours)
대	Vehicles: 자동차 **두 대** (two passenger cars), 트럭 **다섯 대** (five trucks)
장	Pieces of paper: 종이 **한 장** (one piece of paper), 도배지 **열 장** (ten pieces of wallpaper)
권	Books: 책 **여섯 권** (six books)
컵	Beverages that come in a glass: 물 **한 컵** (one glass of water), 주스 **두 컵** (two glasses of juice)

잔	Beverages that come in a small cup or glass: 커피 **한 잔** (*one cup of coffee*), 차 **두 잔** (*two cups of tea*), 소주 **한 잔** (*one shot of soju*)
병	Beverages that come in a bottle: 콜라 **한 병** (*one bottle of cola*), 맥주 **두 병** (*two bottles of beer*)

Listen to Track 61

	Sino-Korean number counters
분	The minutes portion of time: 30분 (*30 minutes*), 40분 (*40 minutes*), 15분 (*15 minutes*), 오후 1시 5분 (*1:05 pm*)
원	Won, the Korean monetary unit: 1,000원 (*1,000 won*), 100,000원 (*100,000 won*). *note: 1,000 won is equivalent to approximately $1.00.
불	American dollar: 1불 (*one dollar*), 10센트 (*ten dollars*)
센트	Cents: 50센트 (*50 cents*), 99센트 (*99 cents*)
번	Assigned number to something: 3번 (*number 3*), 54번 (*number 54*)

You should also be aware that counters for Sino-Korean numbers include the units of measuring weight, length, volume, and distance.

One last thing to mention is that when the native numbers are used with a counter, the numbers 1 to 4 change in format as follows:

Listen to Track 62

#	**Native number**	**When used with a counter**	**Example**
1	하나	한	사과 **한 개** (*one apple*)
2	둘	두	커피 **두 잔** (*two cups of coffee*)
3	셋	세	**세 시** (*3 o'clock*)
4	넷	네	남자 **네 명** (*four men*)

The rest of the numbers remain in their original form even when counters are added.

TIME TO PRACTICE!

A Beginner's Guide to Korean Numbers

Exercise 1. Write down the numbers in native numbers:

1. 22 -> _____
2. 31 -> _____
3. 4 -> _____
4. 14 -> _____
5. 95 -> _____

6. 72 -> _____
7. 99 -> _____
8. 61 -> _____
9. 48 -> _____
10. 6 -> _____

Exercise 2. Write down the numbers in Sino-Korean numbers:

(Note: This is only for the purpose of learning the Sino-Korean numbers in this lesson. In normal situations, you would always write Sino-Korean numbers numerically.)

1. 2,020 -> _____
2. 78,000 -> _____
3. 100,000 -> _____
4. 100,000,000 -> _____
5. 9 -> _____

6. 800 -> _____
7. 77 -> _____
8. 1,000,000 -> _____
9. 4 -> _____
10. 17 -> _____

Exercise 3. Fill in the blanks with Korean counters:

1. 강아지 두 _____ (two puppies) : To count animals
2. 자동차 여섯 _____ (six cars) : To count vehicles
3. 우유 한 _____ (one glass of milk) : To count glasses
4. 맥주 열 _____ (ten bottles of beer) : To count bottles
5. 의자 세 _____ (three chairs) : To count things in general
6. 전단지 백 _____ (a hundred flyers) : To count pages
7. 성인 열 _____ (ten adults) : To count people
8. 교과서 스무 _____ (twenty textbooks) : To count books
9. 오후 다섯 _____ (5 PM) : To indicate the hour
10. 백만 _____ (₩1,000,000) : Korean monetary unit

Exercise 4. Determine if the following sentences are Correct / Incorrect:

1. 가격은 칠백 원이에요. *(It is 700 won.)* _____
2. 집에 한국어 책이 다섯 권 있어요. *(I have 5 Korean books at home.)*
   _____
3. 저는 이십 오 살이에요. *(I am 25 years old.)* _____
4. 둘 더하기 넷은 여섯이에요. *(2 plus 4 is 6.)* _____
5. 지금은 오후 오시 서른분이에요. *(It is 5:30 p.m. now.)* _____
6. 올 해는 이천 이십 년이에요. *(This year is 2020.)* _____
7. 오늘은 제 열 아홉 번째 생일이에요. *(It is my 19th birthday today.)*
   _____
8. 저는 여동생 두 마리가 있어요. *(I have two younger sisters.)* _____
9. 저는 자동차 한 개를 샀어요. *(I bought a car.)* _____
10. 벌써 한 시간이 지났어요. *(It has already been an hour.)* _____

Exercise 5. Determine if the following statements are True / False:

1. You can count "zero" with a native number. _____
2. You can only count to 99 with Sino-Korean numbers. _____
3. You can count "a hundred" with a native number. _____
4. Both 명 and 분 can count people. _____
5. Sino-Korean numbers are based on Chinese characters. _____
6. 100,000,000 is 억 in the Sino-Korean number. _____
7. You should use 장 to count books. _____
8. You can use native numbers for age. _____
9. Native numbers are not based on Chinese characters. _____
10. You should use Sino-Korean numbers for the hour. _____

ANSWERS:

Exercise 1

1. 스물 둘 / 2. 서른 하나 / 3. 넷 / 4. 열 넷 / 5. 아흔 다섯 / 6. 일흔 둘 /
7. 아흔 아홉 / 8. 예순 하나 / 9. 마흔 여덟 / 10. 여섯

Exercise 2

1. 이천 이십 / 2. 칠만 팔천 / 3. 십만 / 4. 억 / 5. 구 / 6. 팔백 / 7. 칠십 칠 /
8. 백만 / 9. 사 / 10. 십 칠

Exercise 3

1. 마리 / 2. 대 / 3. 컵 / 4. 병 / 5. 개 / 6. 장 / 7. 병 / 8. 권 / 9. 시 / 10. 원

Exercise 4

1. Correct / 2. Correct / 3. Incorrect: You should use native numbers for age. /
4. Incorrect: You should use Sino-Korean numbers for calculation. /
5. Incorrect: Sino-Korean numbers for minutes, native numbers for hours. /
6. Correct / 7. Correct / 8. Incorrect: You should use "명" to count people. /
9. Incorrect: You should use "대" to count vehicles. / 10. Correct

Exercise 5

1. False: You cannot count "zero" with native numbers. / 2. False: You can count
beyond 99 with Sino-Korean numbers. / 3. False: You cannot count "a hundred"
with native numbers. / 4. True / 5. True /6. True / 7. False: You should use "권"
to count books. / 8. True / 9. True / 10. False: You should use native numbers for
the hour.

QUICK RECAP

Both the native numbers and the Sino-Korean numbers are used equally as often in the Korean language. The only difference is the situations in which they are used. Having to learn two different number systems at once in a new language can be overwhelming at first.

Start by memorizing the numbers 1 to 20 in both systems, then try practicing saying the numbers in reverse order once you have mastered them in the forward order. Saying the numbers backwards helps you imprint each number in your head instead of just memorizing them in order.

The various counters for different types of nouns are also difficult to master, but it will eventually sink in as you use them more and more.

LESSON 8: MORE ON COUNTERS

In this lesson, you will learn more about the counters we introduced in Lesson 7. Counters are important in Korean, as Korean uses specific words to count different things. Let us look a bit more closely at how counters work in Korean.

The Counters

You might not be familiar with counters as English does not use many of them. While Indo-European languages do not use counters much, many Asian languages including Korean, Japanese, and Chinese use them extensively.

English examples

- A **stick** of gum **(Correct)**
- A **bar** of gum / A **tube** of gum **(Incorrect)**

Although you might understand what "a bar of gum" means, it sounds weird. It is because we did not use the right counter "stick" for the gum. It's not a perfect comparison, due to English not relying on counters as much; however, Korean needs different counters for different words.

There are so many Korean counters that even natives cannot memorize all of them. Thus, today we are going to study the most common ones to count people, animals, and things.

How to Count People

The most important counters are the ones to count people. Imagine that you accidentally use the counter for animals when you're counting people! It could cause more troubles than other counters would. So, it is important to learn how to count people first.

Listen to Track 63

명 to count people

In most cases, you can count people with 명.

- **여자** 열 **명**이 레스토랑으로 들어갔다. (***Ten women*** *entered the restaurant.*)
- **어린이** 이십 **명**이 운동장에서 놀고 있다. (***Twenty children*** *are playing in the playground.*)
- **학생** 삼십 **명**이 교실에서 공부하고 있다. (***Thirty students*** *are studying in the class.*)

Listen to Track 64

분 to count people

You can use 분 to count people when a situation requires formality or politeness, like talking to older people, superiors at a workplace, or strangers at a social event.

- 회의에 일곱 **분** 참석하셨습니다. (*Seven **people** attended the meeting.*)
- 총 몇 **분**이 오실 예정이신가요? (*How many **people** are coming?*)
- 초대받은 서른 **분**만 파티에 참석하실 수 있습니다. (*Only thirty **people** with invitations can join the party.*)

How to Count Animals

Even though there are many counters for each animal, you can just use 마리 to count animals. Besides, the National Institute of Korean Language recommends using 마리 to count animals as it is confusing to use different counters for different animals.

Listen to Track 65

마리 to count animals

- 나는 **고양이** 한 **마리**가 있다. (*I have a cat.*)
- **말** 다섯 **마리**가 달리고 있다. -> **말** 다섯 **필**이 달리고 있다. (*Five horses are running.*)

  You can count horses with 마리, but you can also use more precise numeral classifier 필 for counting horses.
- 나는 **닭** 한 **마리**를 먹었다. (*I ate a chicken.*)

How to Count Things

It can be tiring to try to memorize every counter. While it is true that using various counters will make you sound more native, you can just use 개 to count things for now. Refer to the list provided in this lesson for the most commonly used counters!

Listen to Track 66

개 to count things

- 나는 **손목시계**가 세 **개** 있다. (*I have three watches.*)
- 나는 **책장**이 한 **개** 있다. (*I have a bookshelf.*)
- 나는 **모자**가 한 **개** 있다. (*I have a hat.*)

Listen to Track 67

켤레 and 짝 to count things in pairs

When you count something like socks, shoes, or gloves (which come in pairs), you can use 켤레. You can use 짝 when you indicate just one of a pair of socks, shoes, or gloves.

- **신발** 한 **짝**이 없어졌다. (*One shoe is missing.*)
- 나는 어제 **장갑** 세 **켤레**를 샀다. (*I bought three pairs of gloves yesterday.*)
- 바지 한 **켤레** / 안경 한 **켤레** (**Incorrect**) (*A pair of trousers. / A pair of glasses.*)

While glasses have two lenses and trousers have two legs, Korean does not use 켤레 to count these things. If it is physically connected, you have to use 개 instead of 켤레.

Other Counters

You do not have to memorize every counter. It will be useful, however, if you memorize the following twelve counters, as they are common in modern Korean.

Listen to Track 68

벌	clothes	대	vehicles / machines
채	buildings	권	books
개비	cigarettes	필	horses
그루	trees	통	letters / calls / emails

송이	*flowers / grapes*	병	*bottles*
척	*ships*	잔	*glasses*

The difference between 개 and 대

Listen to Track 69

When you count machines or vehicles, you can use 대 for the whole machine and 개 for its components.

- **컴퓨터** 한 **대** (*a computer*)
- **노트북** 한 **대** (*a laptop computer*)
- **기차** 한 **대** (*a train*)

You can still use 개 to count machines, but it sounds more natural to count complex machines like trains with 대.

- **그래픽카드** 한 **개** (**Correct**) (*a graphics card*)
  그래픽카드 한 **대** (**Incorrect**)

- **타이어** 두 **개** (**Correct**) (*two tires*)
  타이어 두 **대** (**Incorrect**)

- **나사** 삼십 **개** (**Correct**) (*thirty screws*)
  나사 삼십 **대** (**Incorrect**)

A graphics card, a tire, or a screw are components of bigger machines or vehicles. To count these components, you have to use 개.

The Difference Between 잔 (Glass) in Korean and "Glass" in English

While English speakers use "glass" for cold drinks and "cup" for hot drinks, Koreans use "glass" for both hot and cold drinks. In fact, Koreans drink "ice coffee," which is cold coffee with ice. So Koreans do drink "a glass of coffee"!

Listen to Track 70

- **커피** 한 **잔** 마실래? (*Do you want a cup of coffee?*)
- **맥주** 한 **잔** 마시러 가자! (*Let's drink a glass of beer!*)

TIME TO PRACTICE!

More on Counters

Exercise 1. Fill in the blanks with the correct numeral classifier to complete the sentences:

1. 남자 세 _____ 이 식당으로 들어갔다. *(Three men entered the restaurant.)*
2. 학생 열 _____ 이 도서관에서 공부하고 있다. *(Ten students are studying in the library.)*
3. 나는 장갑 한 _____ 를 샀다. *(I bought a pair of gloves.)*
4. 나사 백 _____ 를 주문해라. *(Place an order for a hundred crews.)*
5. 신발 한 _____ 이 사라졌다. *(I lost a shoe.)*
6. 나는 모자가 세 _____ 있다. *(I have three hats.)*
7. 기차 한 _____ 가 다리 위를 지나간다. *(A train passes over a bridge.)*
8. 어린이 다섯 _____ 이 유치원에 있다. *(There are five children in kindergarten.)*
9. 나는 강아지 한 _____ 를 기른다. *(I have a puppy.)*
10. 기린 세 _____ 가 있다. *(There are three giraffes.)*

Exercise 2. Fill in the blanks with the correct numeral classifiers described in the following explanations:

1. To count animals in general (Example) 강아지 세 _____ *(Three puppies)*.
2. To count people in general (Example) 어른 열 _____ *(Ten adults)*.
3. To count people with formality (Example) 일곱 _____ *(Seven people)*.
4. To count things in general (Example) 컵 한 _____ *(A cup)*.
5. To count things in pairs (Example) 양말 한 _____ *(A pair of socks)*.
6. To count one of a pair of shoes (Example) 장갑 한 _____ *(A glove)*.
7. To count machines or vehicles (Example) 자동차 한 _____ *(A car)*.
8. To count trees (Example) 나무 여덟 _____ *(Eight trees)*.
9. To count books (Example) 책 스무 _____ *(Twenty books)*.
10. To count bottles (Example) 와인 두 _____ *(Two bottles of wine)*.

Exercise 3. Choose the right one in the following sentences:

1. 어린이 스무 **[명 / 마리 / 개]** 이 놀이공원으로 들어갔다. *(Twenty children entered the amusement park.)* _____

2. 내 방에는 화분이 한 **[명 / 마리 / 개]** 있다. *(I have a flowerpot in my room.)* _____

3. 의사 세 **[명 / 마리 / 개]** 이 수술 중이다. *(Three doctors are operating.)* _____

4. 늑대 세 **[명 / 마리 / 개]** 가 사슴을 사냥 중이다. *(Three wolves are hunting a deer.)* _____

5. 내 방에는 책상이 한 **[명 / 마리 / 개]** 있다. *(I have a desk in my room.)* _____

6. 나는 여동생이 두 **[명 / 마리 / 개]** 있다. *(I have two younger sisters.)* _____

7. 사자 두 **[명 / 마리 / 개]** 가 낮잠을 자고 있다. *(Two lions are taking a nap.)* _____

8. 나는 모니터가 두 **[명 / 마리 / 개]** 있다. *(I have two monitors.)* _____

9. 아버지는 형제가 세 **[명 / 마리 / 개]** 있다. *(My father has three brothers.)* _____

10. 나는 지우개 두 **[명 / 마리 / 개]** 를 샀다. *(I bought two erasers.)* _____

Exercise 4. Determine if the following sentences are Correct / Incorrect:

1. 나는 형 세 마리가 있다. *(I have three older brothers.)* _____
2. 내 여동생은 인형 세 개를 가지고 있다. *(My sister has three dolls.)* _____
3. 나는 가장 친한 친구 다섯 그루가 있다. *(I have five best friends.)* _____
4. 나는 꽃 한 송이를 친구에게 선물로 주었다. *(I gave a flower to my friend as a gift.)* _____
5. 누나는 새 자동차 한 대를 샀다. *(My sister bought a new car.)* _____
6. 나는 고양이 두 필을 기른다. *(I have two cats.)* _____
7. 나는 책 세 권을 빌렸다. *(I borrowed three books.)* _____
8. 배 세 척이 바다에 떠있다. *(Three ships float in the sea.)* _____
9. 나랑 맥주 한 잔 할래요? *(Do you want to drink a beer with me?)* _____
10. 어머니는 와인 두 병을 꺼냈다. *(My mother took out two bottles of wine.)* _____

Exercise 5. Determine if the following statements are True / False:

1. If you need to be polite, you can use 명 instead of 분. _____
2. For components of machines, you have to use 대 instead of 개. _____
3. 잔 can be used to count cups and glasses. _____
4. You can use 켤레 when you count trousers or glasses. _____
5. 짝 means "a pair" in English. _____
6. To count cigarettes, you can use 개비. _____
7. 송이 can be used to count grapes. _____
8. To count buildings, you can use 채. _____
9. 통 cannot be used to count emails. _____
10. There is no numeral classifier for books. _____

ANSWERS:

Exercise 1

1. 명 / 2. 명 / 3. 켤레 / 4. 개 / 5. 짝 / 6. 개 / 7. 대 / 8. 명 / 9. 마리 / 10. 마리

Exercise 2

1. 마리 / 2. 명 / 3. 분 / 4. 개 / 5. 켤레 / 6. 짝 / 7. 대 / 8. 그루 / 9. 권 / 10. 병

Exercise 3

1. 명 / 2. 개 / 3. 명 / 4. 마리 / 5. 개 / 6. 명 / 7. 마리 / 8. 개 / 9. 명 / 10. 개

Exercise 4

1. Incorrect (마리 -> 명) / 2. Correct / 3. Incorrect (그루 -> 명) / 4. Correct / 5. Correct / 6. Incorrect (필 -> 마리) / 7. Correct / 8. Correct / 9. Correct / 10. Correct

Exercise 5

1. False (분 is the polite form of 명.) / 2. False (For machine components, you can use 개.) / 3. True / 4. False (You can use 켤레 to count socks.) / 5. False (짝 means one of a pair such as a shoe or a sock.) / 6. True / 7. True / 8. True / 9. False (통 can be used to count emails.) / 10. False (The numeral classifier for books is 권.)

QUICK RECAP

In this lesson, you learned about numeral classifiers in Korean. Please check the table of the most common numeral classifiers in Korean. You did an excellent job today!

Listen to Track 71

The Ten Most Common Numeral Classifiers in Korean	
명	To count people
분	To count people (formal)
마리	To count animals
개	To count things
켤레 / 짝	To count things in pairs
대	To count vehicles / machines
그루	To count trees
권	To count books
병	To count glasses
잔	To count bottles

LESSON 9: INTRODUCTION TO TIME, DAYS, WEEKS, AND MONTHS

After you learn the numbers, the next logical step in your Korean journey is to learn about time and dates, since both the native and Sino-Korean numeric systems are used and it is a good way to practice.

| Interesting fact: | *24-hour notation is mostly used in text and it can be written as "15:10" or "15시 10분." Dates can be written as "2022.01.22" or "2022년 01월 22일."* |

Telling the Time

As you know by now, Korean has two number systems and both are used in telling the time. Native numbers are used for hours and Sino-Korean numbers are used for minutes, seconds, and dates.

The following table has a few examples:

Listen to Track 72

Native	Sino-Korean
세 시 3 o'clock	십오 분 15 minutes
여섯 시 6 o'clock	삼십 초 30 seconds
열두 시 12 o'clock	일월 January

Now let's see how they work together in a sentence if you want to say "It is 6:30." in Korean, this is how it works:

Listen to Track 73

여섯 시 삼십분이에요.

- **Hours in Korean**

When counting hours, the native system is used. The way that works is a combination of the native number and 시, which comes from 시간 – the word for time.

Here we have the hours from one to 12 o'clock:

Listen to Track 74

1 o'clock	한시	7 o'clock	일곱 시
2 o'clock	두시	8 o'clock	여덟 시
3 o'clock	세시	9 o'clock	아홉 시
4 o'clock	네시	10 o'clock	열시
5 o'clock	다섯 시	11 o'clock	열한 시
6 o'clock	여섯 시	12 o'clock	열두 시

Let's use one o'clock as an example for analyzing the structure.

Listen to Track 75

한시 = 한 + 시

한: Comes from 하나, meaning *one*.

시: Comes from 시간, meaning *time*.

- **Minutes and seconds in Korean**

Listen to Track 76

Sino numbers are used for minutes and seconds. For minutes you should use 분 and for seconds 초.

일분 = *one minute*

일초 = *one second*

In the following table we have the most commonly used minutes:

Listen to Track 77

5 minutes	오 분	35 minutes	삼십오 분
10 minutes	십분	40 minutes	사십 분
15 minutes	십오 분	45 minutes	사십오 분
20 minutes	이십 분	50 minutes	오십 분
25 minutes	이십오 분	55 minutes	오십오 분
30 minutes	삼십 분		

When counting seconds, you follow the same structure, but with 초 instead of 분.

- **AM/PM in Korean**

Listen to Track 78

When we want to use the 12-hour system we keep the previous system and add 오전 for AM and 오후 for PM.

Here is how that works from 12 PM to 11 PM:

12 PM	오후 열두 시	6 PM	오후 여섯 시
1 PM	오후 한 시	7 PM	오후 일곱 시
2 PM	오후 두 시	8 PM	오후 여덟 시
3 PM	오후 세 시	9 PM	오후 아홉 시
4 PM	오후 네 시	10 PM	오후 열 시
5 PM	오후 다섯 시	11 PM	오후 열한 시

And here from 12 AM to 11 AM :

Listen to Track 79

12 AM	오전 열두 시	6 AM	오전 여섯 시
1 AM	오전 한 시	7 AM	오전 일곱 시
2 AM	오전 두 시	8 AM	오전 여덟 시
3 AM	오전 세시	9 AM	오전 아홉 시
4 AM	오전 네시	10 AM	오전 열 시
5 AM	오전 다섯 시	11 AM	오전 열한 시

• More Specific Ways of Telling Time in Korean

Listen to Track 80

Let's say you want to be more specific than just using 오전 or 오후. You can say:

- Pre-dawn 새벽: used between 1 AM and 6 AM.
- Morning 아침: used between 7 AM and 11 AM.
- Lunch 점심: for noon.
- Afternoon 오후: used between 12 PM and 5 PM, the same as PM.
- Evening 저녁: used between 5 PM and around 9 PM.
- Night 밤: used between sunset and sunrise.

Listen to Track 81

Pre-Dawn	Morning	Evening	Night
1 in the pre-dawn 새벽 한 시	7 in the morning 아침 일곱 시	6 in the evening 저녁 여섯 시	6 at night 밤 여섯 시
2 in the pre-dawn 새벽 두 시	8 in the morning 아침 여덟 시	7 in the evening 저녁 일곱 시	7 at night 밤 일곱 시
3 in the pre-dawn 새벽 세 시	9 in the morning 아침 아홉 시	8 in the evening 저녁 여덟 시	8 at night 밤 여덟 시
4 in the pre-dawn 새벽 네 시	10 in the morning 아침 열 시	9 in the evening 저녁 아홉 시	9 at night 밤 아홉 시
5 in the pre-dawn 새벽 다섯 시	11 in the morning 아침 열한 시	10 in the evening 저녁 열 시	10 at night 밤 열 시
6 in the pre-dawn 새벽 여섯 시		11 in the evening 저녁 열한 시	11 at night 밤 열한 시
			12 at night 밤 열두 시

More Specific Ways of Telling Dates in Korean

Dates in Korean are structured as year, month, and day. Sino-Korean numbers are used for dates.

- ## Years in Korean

Listen to Track 82

When counting years, you need to use the Sino-Korean number before 년 – meaning *year*. It is the opposite of English where we say "*the year 2020*." In Korean we say "2020년."

- ## Months in Korean

Listen to Track 83

Learning the months in Korean is an intuitive process after you learn the Sino-Korean numbers. All you need to do is add 월 – meaning *month* – after the numbers up to 12.

Months of the Year	
January	일월
February	이월
March	삼월
April	사월
May	오월
June	유월
July	칠월
August	팔월
September	구월
October	시월
November	십일월
December	십이월

June and October are special cases where you take one consonant out of the number. 육 becomes 유 and 십 becomes 시.

• Days in Korean

Listen to Track 84

Understanding days in Korean is one of the trickiest things when learning dates and time, as there are multiple words that mean "day" and more than one way of counting days. But after you get the pattern, everything makes sense.

Let's start with counting days. If you are counting from one to ten there is a specific word for each day, but the most commonly used is 하루 (haru)—meaning *one day*. For the rest of the days it is more common to use the following structure:

Sino-Korean number + 일

This is also used for referring to a specific day of the month.

일 means *day* and it's the counter for days, it must never be used alone as its meaning changes if not accompanied by a number. If you want a word to be used alone meaning day, you should use 날.

Examples	
I studied for a day	나는 하루 동안 공부했다
July 2nd	칠월 이일
30 days	삼십일
On that day	그날에

Listen to Track 85

The days of the week always end with 요일, which means *day of the week*.

Days of the Week	
Monday	월요일
Tuesday	화요일
Wednesday	수요일
Thursday	목요일
Friday	금요일
Saturday	토요일
Sunday	일요일

Something that can help to learn the days of the week is learning the meaning of each syllable that comes before 요일.

Listen to Track 86

- 월 = *Moon*
- 화 = *Fire*
- 수 = *Water*
- 목 = *Tree*
- 금 = *Metal*
- 토 = *Earth*
- 일 = *Sun*

TIME TO PRACTICE!

Introduction to Time, Days, Weeks, and Months

Exercise 1. Write down the name of the month in Korean:

1. January : _____
2. February : _____
3. March : _____
4. April : _____
5. May : _____

6. July : _____
7. August : _____
8. September : _____
9. November : _____
10. December : _____

Exercise 2. Write down the name of the day in Korean:

1. Monday : _____
2. Tuesday : _____
3. Wednesday: _____
4. Thursday : _____

5. Friday : _____
6. Saturday : _____
7. Sunday : _____

Exercise 3. Fill in the blanks with the time in Korean as described in the following explanations:

1. It indicates the time between midnight and morning: _____
2. It indicates the morning and breakfast time: _____
3. It indicates the afternoon and lunch time: _____
4. It indicates the evening and dinner time: _____
5. It indicates the late night: _____

Exercise 4. Write down the time in Korean:

1. 1 AM in the pre-dawn: _____
2. 11 PM at night: _____
3. 7 PM in the evening: _____
4. 7 AM in the morning: _____
5. 1 PM in the afternoon: _____

6. 4 AM in the pre-dawn: _____
7. 6 AM in the morning: _____
8. 10 PM at night: _____
9. 9 PM in the evening: _____
10. 2 PM in the afternoon: _____

Exercise 5. Determine if the following statements are TRUE / FALSE:

1. You have to use the native number before "년" when counting years. _____

2. Dates in Korean are structured as year, month, and day. _____

3. Two Korean number systems are based on Chinese characters. _____

4. You must use only the Sino-Korean numbers when telling the time. _____

5. Sino numbers are used for minutes and seconds. _____

6. There is no word to indicate "AM" and "PM" in Korean. _____

7. Korean uses the 24-hour system. _____

8. Sino numbers are used for months. _____

9. You should use "월" to indicate the year. _____

10. You must take one consonant out of the number to indicate June or October. _____

ANSWERS:

Exercise 1

1. 일월 / 2. 이월 / 3. 삼월 / 4. 사월 / 5. 오월 / 6. 칠월 / 7. 팔월 / 8. 구월 / 9. 십일월 / 10. 십이월

Exercise 2

1. 월요일 / 2. 화요일 / 3. 수요일 / 4. 목요일 / 5. 금요일 / 6. 토요일 / 7. 일요일

Exercise 3

1. 새벽 / 2. 아침 / 3. 오후 / 4. 저녁 / 5. 밤

Exercise 4

1. 새벽 한 시 / 2. 밤 열한 시 / 3. 저녁 일곱 시 / 4. 아침 일곱 시 / 5. 오후 한 시 / 6. 새벽 네 시 / 7. 아침 여섯 시 / 8. 밤 열 시 / 9. 저녁 아홉 시 / 10. 오후 두 시

Exercise 5

1. False: You must use the Sino-Korean numbers when telling the time. / 2. True / 3. False: Only Sino-Korean numbers are based on Chinese characters. / 4. False: You can use both Sino-Korean and native numbers when telling the time. / 5. True / 6. False: "오전" means "AM," and the word "오후" means "PM."/ 7. False: Korean uses a 12-hour system./ 8. True / 9. False: You should use "년" to indicate the year. / 10. True

QUICK RECAP

Learning about time and dates in Korean is a lot to take in, so make sure you understand each part of the material before continuing. Something that helps with memorizing is to understand the logic behind the word.

After you understand the structure, remembering becomes easier.

In today's lesson you learned about time, months, days, and days of the week. The main focus was building up on your comprehension of numbers to assimilate how time and dates work in Korean.

You can try writing down the current time and date or your birthday using what you learned here.

Using the knowledge to write something will improve your learning experience!

LESSON 10: KOREAN TENSES – EXPRESSING THE PAST, PRESENT, AND FUTURE

Korean verbs are relatively simple to conjugate once you know the *verb stems* along with the *verb endings* of the different tenses.

In this lesson, we will learn how to determine the stem of a verb and how to add the appropriate endings to make them into past, present, or future tenses. Please note that for the entirety of this lesson, we will only be addressing the polite form of speech. You should be aware that the casual and formal forms of speech will have different verb endings.

A. Korean Status (non-action) Verbs

Let's first look at the infinitive forms of four common non-action verbs. The infinitive form of a verb is also known as the dictionary form, like "to be" and "to eat" in English. Every Korean verb in its infinitive form ends with "다."

Listen to Track 87

Verb (infinitive)	Pronunciation	Translation
이다	[이다]	to be (is, am, are)
아니다	[아니다]	to be not (is not, am not, are not)
있다	[읻따]	to have, to exist
없다	[업따]	to not have, to not exist

Present Tense

The first step to conjugating is to find the stem of each verb. The simple way to find the stem is just take away the syllable "다" at the end.

The verb stem for the above verbs are:

Listen to Track 88

- 이다 —>이
- 아니다—>아니
- 있다—>있
- 없다—>없

Next, determine the verb ending. The present tense of a verb (polite speech only) will end with one of the following:

Listen to Track 89

- -아요 (when the last vowel in the verb stem is ㅏ or ㅗ)
- -어요 (when the last vowel in the verb stem is anything else)

The final step is to add the verb ending to the verb stem as follows: .

Listen to Track 90

- 이 + 어요 = 이어요 (evolved into 이에요 / 예요) = is, am, are
- 아니 + 어요 = 아니어요 (evolved into 아니에요) = is not, am not, are not
- 있 + 어요 = 있어요 [이써요] = exists
- 없 + 어요 = 없어요 [업써요] = does not exist

* Notice that all of the above four stems get the -어요 ending.

Past Tense

The past tense of a verb will end with the following:

Listen to Track 91

- -았어요 (when the last vowel in the verb stem is ㅏ or ㅗ)
- -었어요 (when the last vowel in the verb stem is anything else)

If you know how to use the present tense, the past tense is very easy. Past tense is exactly like present tense, except you add -써요" after the ㅗ or ㅏ.

Present	Past
-아요	-았어요
-어요	-었어요

As you did with the present tense above, just add the appropriate ending to the verb stem:

Listen to Track 92

- 이 + 었어요 = 이었어요 [이어써요] = was, were
- 아니 + 었어요 = 아니었어요 [아니어써요] = was not, were not
- 있 + 었어요 = 있었어요 [이써써요] = existed
- 없 + 었어요 = 없었어요 [업써써요] = did not exist

Future Tense

The verb ending of future tense is as follows:

Listen to Track 93

- ~ㄹ거예요 (when the verb stem ends with a vowel)
- ~을거예요 (when the verb stem ends with a consonant)

Add one of the above to the verb stem:

Listen to Track 94

- 이 + ㄹ거예요 = 일 거예요 [일 꺼예요] = probably will be
- 아니 + ㄹ거예요 = 아닐 거예요 [아닐 꺼예요] = probably will not be
- 있 + 을거예요 = 있을 거예요 [이쓸 꺼예요] = probably will exist
- 없 + 을거예요 = 없을 거예요 [업쓸 꺼예요] = probably will not exist

As you will notice in the definition, the ending ㄹ/일거예요 does not indicate a definite future. Rather, it indicates a *probable* future.

In the Korean language, this is the most common way to talk about the future. Only the past and the present can be described with certainty. This is another interesting characteristic of the Korean language.

Now let's take a look at the present, past, and future tenses together for better reference:

Listen to Track 95

Infinitive	Verb stem	Present	Past	Future
이다	이-	이에요 / 예요	이었어요 [이써써요]	일 거예요 [일 꺼예요]
아니다	아니-	아니에요	아니었어요 [아니어써요]	아닐 거예요 [아닐 꺼예요]
있다 [읻따]	있-	있어요 [이써요]	있었어요 [이써써요]	있을 거예요 [이쓸 꺼예요]
없다 [업따]	없-	없어요 [업써요]	없었어요 [업써써요]	없을 거예요 [업쓸 꺼예요]

B. Korean Action Verbs

Action verbs describe actions that can be done by the subject of the sentence. Let's conjugate the following verbs using the same steps as above. See if you can figure out what the verb stem is for each verb in the table below.

Listen to Track 96

Verb (infinitive)	Verb stem	Translation
하다	?	*to do*
가다	?	*to go*
오다	?	*to come*
먹다	?	*to eat*

Were you able to find the verb stems?

You are correct! All you need to do is take away "다" to get the verb stems 하-, 가-, 오-, and 먹-.

Now let's find the present, past, and future tenses of the above verbs:

Listen to Track 97

Infinitive	Verb stem	Present	Past	Future
하다	하-	해요 (do)	했어요 (did)	할 거예요 (will do)
가다	가-	가요 (go)	갔어요 (went)	갈 거예요 (will go)
오다	오-	와요 (come)	왔어요 (came)	올 거예요 (will come)
먹다	먹-	먹어요 (eat)	먹었어요 [머거써요] (ate)	먹을 거예요 (will eat)
보다	보	봐요 (look)	봤어요 (looked)	볼 거예요 (will look)
살다	살	살아요 (live)	살았어요 (lived)	살 거예요 (will live)
읽다	읽	읽어요 (read)	읽었어요 (read)	읽을 거예요 (will read)

*With the verb 하다 and 가다, if you follow the same pattern, the present tense should be 하아요 and 가아요. Over time, the present tense for those words became 해요 and 가요. While learning, you will encounter other such words that have evolved over time.

Present Continuous Tense

Listen to Track 98

Since we have covered the past, present, and future tenses, there is one more type of commonly used present tense I should mention. **Present continuous** refers to the current state of *doing* the action, like the words *going, coming,* and *eating*.

To make a Korean verb into the present continuous tense, you simply add the ending ~고 있어요.

Let's look at the same four words:

Infinitive	Verb stem	Present continuous
하다	하-	하고 있어요 (doing)
가다	가-	가고 있어요 (going)
오다	오-	오고 있어요 (coming)
먹다	먹-	먹고 있어요 (eating)

You can see that the pattern is pretty straightforward. Notice that the word 있어요 (exists) is included in the present continuous. Translated literally, it means that whatever action you are describing *currently exists*. In other words, the action is happening now!

Here are a few more action verbs. See if you can come up with the verb tenses:

Infinitive	Stem	Present	Past	Future	Present continuous
마시다 (to drink)					
자다 (to sleep)					
놀다 (to play)					
읽다 (to read)					

How did you do?

Here are the answers:

Listen to Track 99

Infinitive	Stem	Present	Past	Future	Present continuous
마시다	마-	마셔요	마셨어요 [마셔써요]	마실 거예요 [마실 꺼예요]	마시고 있어요 [마시고 이써요]
자다	자-	자요	잤어요 [자써요]	잘 거예요 [잘 꺼예요]	자고 있어요 [자고 이써요]

놀다	놀-	놀아요 [노라요]	놀았어요 [노라써요]	놀 거예요 [놀 꺼예요]	놀고 있어요 [놀고 이써요]
읽다	읽-	읽어요 [일거요]	읽었어요 [일거써요]	읽을 거예요 [일글 꺼예요]	읽고 있어요 [일꼬 이써요]

It wasn't too difficult, right? Great job!!

Let's now look at the verbs used in complete sentences:

Listen to Track 100

Sentence	Pronunciation	Translation
어제는 친구하고 **놀았어요.**	[어제는 칭구하고 노라써요]	Yesterday, I **played** with a friend.
저는 요즘 소설을 **읽고 있어요.**	[저는 요즘 소서를 일꼬 이써요]	These days, I'm **reading** a novel.
오빠가 맥주를 너무 많이 **마셨어요.**	[오빠가 맥쭈를 너무 마니 마셔써요]	My brother **drank** too much beer.
우리 남편은 지금 **자고 있어요.**	[우리 남펴는 지금 자고 이써요]	My husband is **sleeping** right now.
그 편지는 이따 **읽을 거예요.**	[그 편지는 이따 일글 꺼예요]	I **will read** that letter later.

Korean action verbs combining a noun with the verb "Do"

The last topic that I want to introduce in this article involves the Korean verb "하다" (*do*). There are many nouns that are combined with 하다 to become action verbs.

Listed below are some examples of this combination:

Listen to Track 101

Noun	Translation	+ 하다 (infinitive verb)	Translation
공부	*study*	공부하다	*to study*
생각	*thought(s)*	생각하다	*to think*
일	*work*	일하다	*to work*
운동	*exercise*	운동하다	*to exercise*
요리	*cooking (a dish that has been cooked)*	요리하다	*to cook*

In order to determine the various tenses of these verbs, refer back to the verb " 하다":

Listen to Track 102

Infinitive	Verb stem	Present	Past	Future
하다	하-	해요	했어요 [해써요]	할 거예요 [할 꺼예요]

Listen to Track 103

Infinitive	Verb stem	Present	Past	Future
이다	이-	이에요 / 예요	이었어요 [이어써요]	일 거예요 [일 꺼예요]
아니다	아니-	아니에요	아니었어요 [아니어써요]	아닐 거예요 [아닐 꺼예요]
있다 [읻따]	있-	있어요 [이써요]	있었어요 [이써써요]	있을 거예요 [이쓸 꺼예요]
없다 [업따]	없-	없어요 [업써요]	없었어요 [업써써요]	없을 거예요 [업쓸 꺼예요]

TIME TO PRACTICE!

Korean Tenses – Expressing the Past, Present, and Future

Exercise 1. Fill in the blanks to transform the sentences to its future tense form:

1. 나는 집에서 음악을 들어요. -> 나는 집에서 음악을 _____.
    (I listen to music at home. -> I will listen to music at home.)

2. 나는 아침에 조깅을 해요. -> 나는 아침에 조깅을 _____.
    (I go jogging in the morning. -> I will go jogging in the morning.)

3. 나는 저녁에 삼겹살을 먹어요. -> 나는 저녁에 삼겹살을 _____.
    (I eat Korean BBQ for dinner. -> I will eat Korean BBQ for dinner.)

4. 나는 친구들과 게임을 해요. -> 나는 친구들과 게임을 _____.
    (I play video games with my friends. -> I will play video games with my friends.)

5. 나는 영어 시험을 봐요. -> 나는 영어 시험을 _____.
    (I have an English exam. -> I will have an English exam.)

6. 나는 한국어 수업에 가요. -> 나는 한국어 수업에 _____.
    (I go to Korean class. -> I will go to Korean class.)

7. (여)동생은 다음 달에 11살이 되요. -> (여)동생은 다음 달에 11살이 _____.
    (My sister turns 11 years old next month. -> My sister will turn 11 years old next month.)

8. 금 가격이 크게 올라요. -> 금 가격이 크게 _____.
    (Gold prices rise significantly. -> Gold prices will rise significantly.)

9. 복지 정책이 확대 되요. -> 복지 정책이 확대 _____.
    (Welfare policies are expanded. -> Welfare policies will be expanded.)

10. 도시는 더욱 안전해져요. -> 도시는 더욱 안전_____.
    (The city becomes safer. -> The city will become safer.)

Exercise 2. Fill in the blanks to transform the sentences into its past tense form:

1. 나는 후회스러운 일을 해요. -> 나는 후회스러운 일을 _____.
   (*I do something regrettable. -> I did something regrettable.*)

2. 나는 잠을 푹 자요. -> 나는 잠을 푹_____.
   (*I sleep well. -> I slept well.*)

3. 나는 한국어 자격증을 취득해요. -> 나는 한국어 자격증을 취득_____.
   (*I'm getting the Korean certification. -> I got the Korean certification.*)

4. 실업률이 크게 증가해요. -> 실업률이 크게 증가_____.
   (*The unemployment rate rises greatly. -> The unemployment rate rose greatly.*)

5. 나는 TV에서 내 친구를 봐요. -> 나는 TV에서 내 친구를 _____.
   (*I see my friend on TV. -> I saw my friend on TV.*)

6. 나는 터키에서 여름 휴가를 보내요. -> 나는 터키에서 여름 휴가를 _____.
   (*I have a summer vacation in Turkey. -> I had a summer vacation in Turkey.*)

7. 서울에 큰 축제가 열려요. -> 서울에 큰 축제가 _____.
   (*A big festival is held in Seoul. -> A big festival was held in Seoul.*)

8. 나는 그 소식을 듣고 매우 기뻐요. -> 나는 그 소식을 듣고 매우 _____.
   (*I am delighted to hear that. -> I was delighted to hear that.*)

9. 두 나라는 휴전을 해요. -> 두 나라는 휴전을 _____.
   (*The two countries sign a truce. -> The two countries signed a truce.*)

10. 그는 끝까지 포기하지 않아요. -> 그는 끝까지 포기하지 _____.
    (*He never gives up. -> He never gave up.*)

Exercise 3. Fill in the blanks in the following sentences:

1. 나는 매일 비타민 D를 _____. (Verb stem: 먹-)
   (*I take a vitamin D pill every day.*)

2. 나는 동생과 수영장에 _____. (Verb stem: 가-)
   (*I went to the pool with my brother.*)

3. 태양은 동쪽에서 _____. (Verb stem: 뜨-)
   (*The sun rises from the east.*)

4. 나는 그 사람을 꼭 _____. (Verb stem: 찾-)
   (*I will find that person.*)

5. 두 국가의 외교관이 서로 _____. (Verb stem: 만나-)
   (The diplomats from both countries met with each other.)

6. 작년부터 관세가 인하 _____. (Verb stem: 되-)
   (Tariffs have been reduced since last year.)

7. 누나는 주말마다 프랑스어를 _____. (Verb stem: 공부하-)
   (My sister studies French every weekend.)

8. 취업률이 빠르게 _____. (Verb stem: 증가하-)
   (The employment rate will rise quickly.)

9. 고양이는 매일 낮잠을 _____. (Verb stem: 자-)
   (My cat takes a nap every day.)

10. 나는 내일 영화관에 _____. (Verb stem: 가-)
    (I will go to the cinema tomorrow.)

Exercise 4. Determine if the following sentences are Correct / Incorrect:

1. 나는 내일 학교에 갔어요. *(I went to school.)* _____
2. 나는 어제 친구들과 놀 거예요. *(I hung out with friends yesterday.)* _____
3. 매일 아침 나는 토마토를 먹어요. *(I eat a tomato every morning.)* _____
4. 지구는 태양 주변을 돌 거예요. *(The Earth revolves around the sun.)* _____
5. 나는 스위스에서 겨울 휴가를 보내요. *(I had a winter vacation in Switzerland.)* _____
6. 저번 주에 환율이 하락할 거예요. *(The exchange rate fell last week.)* _____
7. 나는 어제 새로운 안경을 사러 갔어요. *(I went out to buy new glasses.)* _____
8. 나는 클래식 음악을 좋아해요. *(I like classical music.)* _____
9. 동생은 일주일에 한 번씩 자원봉사를 해요. *(My brother volunteers once a week.)* _____
10. 나는 이번 주말에 부산에 갔어요. *(I will go to Busan this weekend.)* _____

Exercise 5. Check if the following statements are True / False:

1. The infinitive of a verb is identical to the present form of a verb. _____
2. For the present tense, you do not have to modify the infinitive of a verb. _____
3. The infinitive of a verb is typically the basic form of a verb without "다." _____
4. "이다," "아니다," "있다," and "없다" are examples of action verbs. _____
5. The ending "일 거에요" indicates a probable future. _____
6. "았어요" and "었어요" are future tense endings. _____
7. You can combine a noun with the verb "하다." _____
8. "어요" and "아요" are past tense endings. _____
9. "할 거에요" is the future tense of the verb "하다." _____
10. "하다," "가다," "오다," and "먹다" are examples of action verbs. _____

ANSWERS:

Exercise 1

1. 들을 거예요 / 2. 할 거예요 / 3. 먹을 거예요 / 4. 할 거예요 / 5. 볼 거예요 /
6. 갈 거예요 / 7. 될 거예요 / 8. 오를 거예요 / 9. 될 거예요 / 10. 해질거예요

Exercise 2

1. 했어요 / 2. 잤어요 / 3. 했어요 / 4. 했어요 / 5. 봤어요 / 6. 보냈어요 /
7. 열렸어요 / 8. 기뻤어요 / 9. 했어요 / 10. 않았어요

Exercise 3

1. 먹어요 / 2. 갔어요 / 3. 떠요 / 4.찾을 거예요 / 5. 만났어요 /
6. 되었어요(됐어요) / 7. 공부해요 / 8. 증가할 거예요 / 9. 자요 / 10. 갈 거예요

Exercise 4

1. Incorrect: "내일" means "tomorrow." You cannot use it in a past tense sentence. / 2. Incorrect: "놀 거예요" is future tense. "놀았어요" should be used for the past tense. / 3. Correct / 4. Incorrect: "돌 거예요" is future tense. "돌아요" should be used for the present tense. / 5. Correct / 6. Incorrect: "하락할 거예요" is future tense. "하락했어요" should be used for past tense. / 7. Correct / 8. Correct / 9. Correct / 10. Incorrect: "갔어요" is the past tense form of "가다." The future tense is 갈 거예요.

Exercise 5

1. False: The infinitive of a verb is not identical to the present tense of a verb. /
2. False: You should modify the infinitive of a verb to indicate tense. / 3. True /
4. False: "이다," "아니다," "있다," and "없다" are examples of non-action verbs. /
5. True / 6. False: "았어요" and "었어요" are past tense endings. / 7. True /
8. False: "어요" and "아요" are present tense endings. /9. True / 10. True

QUICK RECAP

In this lesson, we learned the past, present, and future tenses of several status verbs and action verbs. We have introduced only a few of the verb endings that exist in the Korean language. There are many more verb endings still to learn, but you are now on your way to mastering the past, present, and future!

As you continue to increase your vocabulary, you should get in the habit of learning the different conjugations of each verb that you add to your list. Eventually, the verb tenses will become second nature to you as you compose your sentences!

CHAPTER "GOOD WILL"

Helping others without expectation of anything in return has been proven to lead to increased happiness and satisfaction in life.

We would love to give you the chance to experience that same feeling during your reading or listening experience today...

All it takes is a few moments of your time to answer one simple question:

> **Would you make a difference in the life of someone you've never met—without spending any money or seeking recognition for your good will?**

If so, we have a small request for you.

If you've found value in your reading or listening experience today, we humbly ask that you take a brief moment right now to leave an honest review of this book. It won't cost you anything but 30 seconds of your time—just a few seconds to share your thoughts with others.

Your voice can go a long way in helping someone else find the same inspiration and knowledge that you have.

Scan the QR code below:

OR

Visit the link below:

https://geni.us/DXAIx

Thank you in advance!

LESSON 11: AN EASY GUIDE TO KOREAN ADJECTIVES

As we all know, an adjective describes a noun. In sentences, we often see two different ways an adjective is used. It can be used after a "to be" verb to describe the subject, or it can come before the noun that it is describing.

Here is an example using the word *cold:*

A. The weather is **cold**.

B. The **cold** weather keeps me indoors.

Korean adjectives can also be used in two different ways.

In this article, we will go over the difference between Korean adjectives that come at the end of a sentence (like in Example A) and adjectives that precede the nouns that they modify (like in Example B).

Adjectives that precede the nouns they modify are called attributive adjectives, and adjectives that come at the end of the sentence (and act as verbs) are called predicative adjectives.

Korean Adjectives That Are Also Verbs

When a Korean adjective comes at the end of a sentence, it is a predicative adjective that takes on the characteristics of a verb. A verb-like adjective can also be conjugated like any other verb by using the appropriate endings.

*For more information about verb endings, please refer to the previous lesson on verb tenses, "A Simple Guide to Verb Tenses: Past, Present, and Future."

Let's look at some examples using words that describe the weather.

Listen to Track 104

Verb-like adjective (infinitive)	Pronunciation	Translation
춥다	[춥따]	*To be cold*
덥다	[덥따]	*To be hot*
따뜻하다	[따뜨타다]	*To be warm*
시원하다	[시워나다]	*To be cool / refreshing*

As we mentioned above, because the adjectives are also verbs, you can add verb endings to the stems to make them past, present, or future.

Listen to Track 105

Infinitive	Present tense	Past tense	Future tense
춥다	추워요 *(it is cold)*	추웠어요 [추워써요] *(it was cold)*	추울거예요 [추울꺼예요] *(it will probably be cold)*
덥다	더워요 *(it is hot)*	더웠어요 [더워써요] *(it was hot)*	더울거예요 [더울꺼예요] *(it will probably be hot)*
따뜻하다	따뜻해요 [따뜨태요] *(it is warm)*	따뜻했어요 [따뜨태써요] *(it was warm)*	따뜻할거예요 [따뜨탈꺼예요] *(it will probably be warm)*
시원하다	시원해요 [시워내요] *(it is cool)*	시원했어요 [시워내써요] *(it was cool)*	시원할거예요 [시워날꺼예요] *(it will probably be cool / refreshing)*

Let's take a look at some example sentences using the above verb-like adjectives.

Listen to Track 106

Sentence	Pronunciation	Translation
오늘은 날씨가 **따뜻해요.**	[오느른 날씨가 따뜨태요]	*Today, the weather is warm.*

어제는 날씨가 **추웠어요.**	[어제는 날씨가 추워써요]	*Yesterday, the weather was cold.*
내일은 날씨가 **더울거예요.**	[내이른 날씨가 더울꺼예요]	*Tomorrow, the weather will probably be hot.*

Korean Adjectives That Come Before Nouns

In the above examples, the adjective (also verb) ends the sentence and is the main information that is being conveyed about the weather.

When the adjective precedes a noun that it describes, it is an attributive adjective that takes on the consonant "ㄴ" as its ending and becomes a part of the subject or the object of the sentence. More information (including another verb) is then needed to complete the sentence.

Let's look at how it looks in practice, using the same four words:

Listen to Track 107

- 춥다: 추우 + ㄴ = 추운(cold)
- *덥다: 더우 + ㄴ = 더운 (hot)
- 따뜻하다: 따뜨하 + ㄴ = 따뜻한 [따뜨탄] (warm)
- 시원하다: 시원하 + ㄴ = 시원한 [시워난] (cool)

> *Note: Verb stems that end in the consonant ㅂ conjugate differently. Please refer to the appendix section Sound Change Rules for more information.
>
> Once this change has been made, the words can no longer stand on their own. Adding the "ㄴ" indicates that there is a noun that follows immediately thereafter.

Listen to Track 108

- 추운 날씨 *(cold weather)*
- 더운 공기 *(hot air)*
- 따뜻한 담요 *(warm blanket)*
- 시원한 바람 *(cool wind)*

The two words together will then be either the subject or the object of a sentence.

Listen to Track 109

- 저는 **추운 날씨**를 좋아해요 [저는 추운 날씨를 조아해요].
  *I like **cold weather**.* ("Cold weather" is the object of the sentence.)

- 요즘 **추운 날**들이 너무 많아요 [요즘 추운 날드리 너무 마나요].

*These days, there are too many **cold days**.* ("Cold days" is the subject of the sentence — literally translated, the sentence reads, *"These days, cold days are too many."*)

*많아요 (many) is a verb-like adjective, and 너무 (too) is an adverb for 많아요.

To simplify the difference between the two types of adjectives:

- If you use an adjective with a "to be" verb ending, you get a descriptive verb that ends the sentence.
- If you add the consonant "ㄴ" to the word stem, the adjective describes a noun that follows it.

Below is a list of adjectives (including the four given above) for you to use as a reference:

A list of 20 common Korean adjectives

Listen to Track 110

Adjective	Verb-like adjective	Adjective before a noun
춥다 [춥따] *to be cold*	추워요 *is/am/are cold*	추운 *cold (+noun)*
덥다 [덥따] *to be hot*	더워요 *is/am/are hot*	더운 *hot (+noun)*
따뜻하다 [따뜨타다] *to be warm*	따뜻해요 [따뜨태요] *is/am/are warm*	따뜻한 [따뜨탄] *warm (+noun)*
시원하다 [시워나다] *to be cool / refreshing*	시원해요 [시워내요] *is/ am/are cool / refreshing*	시원한 [시워난] *cool / refreshing (+noun)*
좋다 [조타] *to be good*	좋아요 [조아요] *is/am/are good*	좋은 [조은] *good (+noun)*

나쁘다 *to be bad*	나빠요 *is/am/are bad*	나쁜 *bad (+noun)*
크다 *to be big*	커요 *is/am/are big*	큰 *big (+noun)*
작다 [작따] *to be small*	작아요 [자가요] *is/am/are small*	작은 [자근] *small (+noun)*
길다 *to be long*	길어요 [기러요] *is/am/are long*	긴 [긴] *long (+noun)*
짧다 [짤따] *to be short*	짧아요 [짤바요] *is/am/are short*	짧은 [짤븐] *short (+noun)*

Listen to Track 111

싸다 *to be cheap*	싸요 *is/am/are cheap*	싼 *cheap (+noun)*
비싸다 *to be expensive*	비싸요 *is/am/are expensive*	비싼 *expensive (+noun)*
기쁘다 *to be glad, to be joyful*	기뻐요 *is/am/are glad, joyful*	기쁜 *joyful (+noun)*
슬프다 *to be sad*	슬퍼요 *is/am/are sad*	슬픈 *sad (+noun)*
행복하다 [행보카다] *to be happy*	행복해요 [행보캐요] *am/are happy*	행복한 [행보칸] *happy (+noun)*
아프다 *to hurt, to be sick*	아파요 *is/am/are sick, painful*	아픈 *painful (+noun)*
예쁘다 *to be pretty*	예뻐요 *is/am/are pretty*	예쁜 *pretty (+noun)*
멋있다 *to be cool/stylish*	멋있어요 *is/am/are cool/stylish*	멋있는 *cool/stylish (+noun)*
맛있다 [마싯따] *to taste good*	맛있어요 [마시써요] *tastes good*	맛있는 [마신는] *delicious (+noun)*
맛없다 [마덥따] *to taste bad*	맛없어요 [마덥써요] *tastes bad*	맛없는 [마덤는] *bad tasting (+noun)*
재밌다 [재믿따] *to be fun/interesting*	재밌어요 [재미써요] *is/am/are fun/interesting*	재밌는 [재민는] *fun/interesting (+noun)*

Listen to Track 112

> ***Interesting fact:**
>
> The last three words in the above list are actually full sentences that have evolved into adjectives. If you look closely, they end in "있다" (*to exist*) or "없다" (*to not exist*).
>
> - 맛이 있어요. → 맛있어요. *(Tastes good)*
>   Literally translated: "Taste does exist."
>
> - 맛이 없어요. → 맛없어요. *(Tastes bad)*
>   Literally translated: "Taste does not exist."
>
> - 재미가 있어요. → 재밌어요. *(is fun/interesting)*
>   Literally translated: "Fun does exist."

Listen to Track 113

Knowing that "재밌어요" means something is fun or interesting, can you guess how you would say that something is NOT fun or interesting?

You are right! You would say "재미 없어요." And you would use "재미없는" in front of a noun!

Let's look at some more examples of the two different types of adjectives in full sentences.

Listen to Track 114

Examples of Korean adjectives in sentences:

- 저 남자는 키가 **커요**. *(That man is **tall**.)*
- 저는 키 **큰** 남자를 좋아해요 [저는 키 큰 남자를 조아해요]. *(I like **tall** men.)*
- 이 영화는 **슬퍼요** [이 영화는 슬퍼요]. *(This movie is **sad**.)*
- 어제 **슬픈** 영화를 봤어요 [어제 슬픈 영화를 봐써요]. *(I watched a **sad** movie yesterday.)*
- 비행기 표가 너무 **비싸요**. *(The airline ticket is too **expensive**.)*
- **비싼** 물건이 가격 값을 해요 [비싼 물거니 가격 깝쓸 해요]. (***Expensive** items are worth the price.)*
- 저는 오늘 너무 **행복해요** [저는 오늘 너무 행보캐요]. *(I am so **happy** today.)*

- 올해는 **행복한** 날들이 많기를 바라요 [올해는 행보칸 날드리 만키를 바라요]. *(I hope there will be many **happy** days this year.)*
- 이 에피소드가 아주 **재밌어요** [이 에피쏘드가 아주 재미써요]. *(This episode is very **interesting/fun**.)*
- 우리는 하루 종일 **재미없는** 대화만 했어요 [우리는 하루 종일 재미엄는 대화만 해써요]. *(We had **uninteresting** discussions all day today.)*

TIME TO PRACTICE!

An Easy Guide to Korean Adjectives

Exercise 1. Convert the following adjectives into attributive forms:

Example: 춥다 *(To be cold)* -> 추운 *(Cold)*

1. 덥다 *(To be hot)* -> _____ *(Hot)*
2. 따뜻하다 *(To be warm)* -> _____ *(Warm)*
3. 시원하다 *(To be cool)* -> _____ *(Cool)*
4. 좋다 *(To be good)* -> _____ *(Good)*
5. 나쁘다 *(To be bad)* -> _____ *(Bad)*
6. 크다 *(To be big)* -> _____ *(Big)*
7. 작다 *(To be small)* -> _____ *(Small)*
8. 짧다 *(To be short)* -> _____ *(Short)*
9. 싸다 *(To be cheap)* -> _____ *(Cheap)*
10. 비싸다 *(To be expensive)* -> _____ *(Expensive)*

Exercise 2. Convert the following adjectives into predicative forms:

Example: 기쁜 *(Joyful)* -> 기쁘다 *(To be joyful)*

1. 슬픈 *(Sad)* -> _____ *(To be sad)*
2. 행복한 *(Happy)* -> _____ *(To be happy)*
3. 아픈 *(Sick)* -> _____ *(To be sick)*
4. 예쁜 *(Beautiful)* -> _____ *(To be Beautiful)*
5. 넓은 *(Wide)* -> _____ *(To be wide)*
6. 좁은 *(Narrow)* -> _____ *(To be narrow)*
7. 얇은 *(Thin)* -> _____ *(To be thin)*
8. 굵은 *(Thick)* -> _____ *(To be thick)*
9. 강한 *(Strong)* -> _____ *(To be strong)*
10. 약한 *(Weak)* -> _____ *(To be weak)*

Exercise 3. Find adjectives in the following sentences:

1. 오늘 날씨는 매우 따뜻하다. -> Adjective: _____
   (It is very warm today.)

2. 차가운 주스를 마시고 싶다. -> Adjective: _____
   (I want some cold juice.)

3. 냄비가 너무 뜨거워! -> Adjective: _____
   (The pot is too hot!)

4. 드레스가 정말 예쁘다. -> Adjective: _____
   (The dress is really pretty.)

5. 나는 행복하다. -> Adjective: _____
   (I am happy.)

6. 도둑질은 나빠요. -> Adjective: _____
   (Stealing is bad.)

7. 이 바지는 너무 짧다. -> Adjective: _____
   (These pants are too short.)

8. 그 영화 배우는 멋있다. -> Adjective: _____
   (The actor is stylish.)

9. 내 동생은 감기에 걸려서 아프다. -> Adjective: _____
   (My brother is sick because he has a cold.)

10. 내 고양이는 작다. -> Adjective: _____
    (My cat is small.)

Exercise 4. Determine if the following adjectives are Attributive / Predicative:

1. 날카롭다 *(Sharp / To be sharp)*: [Attributive / Predicative]
2. 낮다 *(Low / To be low)*: [Attributive / Predicative]
3. 무거운 *(Heavy / To be heavy)*: [Attributive / Predicative]
4. 부드럽다 *(Soft / To be soft)*: [Attributive / Predicative]
5. 늦은 *(Late / To be late)*: [Attributive / Predicative]
6. 깊다 *(Deep / To be deep)*: [Attributive / Predicative]
7. 얕다 *(Shallow / To be shallow)*: [Attributive / Predicative]
8. 덥다 *(Hot / To be hot)*: [Attributive / Predicative]
9. 느린 *(Slow / To be slow)*: [Attributive / Predicative]
10. 빠르다 *(Fast / To be fast)*: [Attributive / Predicative]

Exercise 5. Determine if the underlined adjectives are Attributive / Predicative:

1. 그 영화는 **무섭다**. [Attributive / Predicative]
   (The movie is scary.)

2. 이 그림은 매우 **아름답다**. [Attributive / Predicative]
   (This painting is really beautiful.)

3. **따뜻한** 차 한 잔 마시고 싶다. [Attributive / Predicative]
   (I want some hot tea.)

4. 서울에는 **높은** 빌딩이 많다. [Attributive / Predicative]
   (There are many tall buildings in Seoul.)

5. 이 라면은 너무 **맵다**. [Attributive / Predicative]
   (This ramen is too spicy.)

6. 우리는 이 **무거운** 상자들을 옮겨야 한다. [Attributive / Predicative]
   (We have to move these heavy boxes.)

7. 더 **짧은** 바지는 없나요? [Attributive / Predicative]
   (Do you have shorter pants?)

8. 내 강아지는 매우 **작다**. [Attributive / Predicative]
   (My puppy is really small.)

9. 거북이는 **느리다**. [Attributive / Predicative]
   (Turtles are slow.)

10. 느린 거북이와 **빠른** 토끼가 경주를 하고 있다. [Attributive / Predicative]
    (The slow turtle and the fast rabbit are racing.)

ANSWERS:

Exercise 1

1. 더운 / 2. 따뜻한 / 3. 시원한 / 4. 좋은 / 5. 나쁜 / 6. 큰 / 7. 작은 / 8. 짧은 / 9. 싼 / 10. 비싼

Exercise 2

1. 슬프다 / 2. 행복하다 / 3. 아프다 / 4. 예쁘다 / 5. 넓다 / 6. 좁다 / 7. 얇다 / 8. 굵다 / 9. 강하다 / 10. 약하다

Exercise 3

1. 따뜻하다 / 2. 차가운 / 3. 뜨거워 (뜨겁다) / 4. 예쁘다 / 5. 행복하다 / 6. 나빠요 (나쁘다) / 7. 짧다 / 8. 멋있다 / 9. 아프다 / 10. 작다

Exercise 4

1. Predicative / 2. Predicative / 3. Attributive / 4. Predicative / 5. Attributive / 6. Predicative / 7. Predicative / 8. Predicative / 9. Attributive / 10. Predicative

Exercise 5

1. 무섭다 (To be scary): Predicative / 2. 아름답다 (To be beautiful): Predicative / 3. 따뜻한 (Warm): Attributive / 4. 높은 (High/Tall): Attributive / 5. 맵다 (To be spicy): Predicative / 6. 무거운 (Heavy): Attributive / 7. 짧은 (Short): Attributive / 8. 작다 (To be small): Predicative / 9. 느리다 (To be slow): Predicative / 10. 빠른 (Fast): Attributive

QUICK RECAP

Below is a recap of what we have learned in this lesson using several of the adjectives:

Listen to Track 115

Adjective	Used like a verb	Used before a noun
춥다 *to be cold*	날씨가 추워요. *The weather is cold.*	저는 추운 날씨가 싫어요. *I dislike the cold weather.*
덥다 *to be hot*	오늘은 너무 더워요. *Today is too hot.*	더운날씨는 냉면 먹기에 좋아요. *Hot weather is good for eating cold noodles.*
크다 *to be big*	그 남자는 키가 커요. *That man is tall.**	큰 상자 하나가 필요해요. *I need a big box.*
작다 *to be small*	옷이 너무 작아요. *The clothes are too small.*	저는 작은 강아지들을 좋아해요. *I like small puppies.*

*Note: When paired with the word for height 키, 크다 takes on the meaning of "tall."

Here are additional common adjectives introduced in the lesson:

Listen to Track 116

따뜻하다 *to be warm*	시원하다 *to be cool*	좋다 *to be good*	나쁘다 *to be bad*	길다 *to be long*	짧다 *to be short*
싸다 *to be cheap*	비싸다 *to be expensive*	기쁘다 *to be glad*	행복하다 *to be happy*	슬프다 *to be sad*	아프다 *to be sick/ hurt*
예쁘다 *to be pretty*	멋있다 *to be cool/ stylish*	맛있다 *to taste good*	맛없다 *to taste bad*	재밌다 *to be fun/ interesting*	재미없다 *to be boring/ uninteresting*

You should try making your own sentences using the list of common adjectives. In time, you will gradually add even more adjectives to your vocabulary!

LESSON 12: SENTENCE STRUCTURE AND 좋다 VS. 좋아하다

Listen to Track 117

In this lesson, you will learn about the differences between the adjective 좋다 and the verb 좋아하다. The adjective 좋다 means the adjective "good" and the verb 좋아하다 means the verb "to like." Let's look at the differences between the two words in detail.

> **Note:** *You are going to learn again about the* Subject (-은/-는) + Subject (-이/-가) + Adjective (좋다) *structure. Though many Korean grammar points correspond with their English counterparts, this structure is unique and hard to explain in English. So simply note that the* Subject (-은/-는) + Subject (-이/-가) + Adjective (좋다) *structure exists in Korean.*

The Adjective 좋다

The adjective 좋다 means the adjective "good" in English. When you use the adjective 좋다 to mean "good," it is easy to use it. You will get confused, however, when you find out the adjective 좋다 also means the verb "to like." Let us see how we can use the adjective 좋다 in sentences.

How to Use the Adjective 좋다

Listen to Track 118

Structure	Meaning
Subject (-이/-가) + Adjective (좋다)	Subject is good.
Subject A (-은/-는) + Subject B (-이/-가) + Adjective (좋다)	Subject A likes Subject B.

When the adjective 좋다 means the adjective "good"

Listen to Track 119

It is easy to use the adjective 좋다 when it means the adjective "good." You can use it after a subject or other parts of speech combined with nouns and pronouns.

- 이 신발은 좋다. *(These shoes **are good**.)*
- 이 약은 몸에 좋다. *(This medicine **is good** for your health.)*

The basic structure is "이 약은 좋다," meaning "this medicine is good." The adverb "몸에" is inserted between the subject "이 약은" and the adjective "좋다."

- 그녀의 그림 실력**이 좋다**. *(Her drawing skills **are good**.)*

> **Note:** *Korean verbs are placed at the end of sentences. Other adverbs and adjectives, which modify nouns and pronouns, can be inserted between subjects and verbs or adjectives.*

When the adjective 좋다 means the verb "to like"

It is confusing that a subject works like an object when we use the adjective 좋다 to mean the verb "to like." You might not have seen the "subject A + subject B + adjective (좋다)" structure before. There are some structures which natives can understand but are confusing to learners. Let us look at an English sentence.

- *It is important for you to understand this grammar.*

The relationship between the word "you" and the word "understand" in this sentence is that of a subject to its verb. But neither is the subject or verb in this sentence — the actual subject is "it" and the verb is "is").

Now you can get a sense of how the *subject A + subject B + adjective (좋다)* structure works. The subject B is a grammatical subject, but it works like an object. 좋다 (good) is a grammatical adjective, but it works like a verb (like) in this structure. Let's see some examples of how you can use it in sentences.

- 나는 네가 좋다. *(I **like** you.) (As for me, you are good.)*
  Subject A (나는) + Subject B (네가) + Adjective (좋다) = Subject A *likes* Subject B.

- 나는 게임이 좋다. *(I **like** video games. (As for me, video games are good.)*
  Subject A (나는) + Subject B (게임이) + Adjective (좋다) = Subject A *likes* Subject B.

- 나는 삼겹살이 좋다. *(I **like** Korean BBQ.) (As for me, Korean BBQ is good.)*
  Subject A (나는) + Subject B (삼겹살이) + Adjective (좋다) = Subject A *likes* Subject B.

When you cannot use the adjective 좋다:

The adjective 좋다 cannot be used after objects.

Although the adjective 좋다 works like the verb "to like," it is still an adjective. Unlike the verb 좋아하다, the adjective 좋다 cannot be used after object.

- 나는 너를 좋아한다. **(Correct)** *(I **like** you.)*
  나는 너를 좋다. **(Incorrect)**
  The adjective 좋다 cannot be used after the object "너를."

- 내 동생은 게임을 좋아한다. **(Correct)** *(My brother **likes** video games.)*
  내 동생은 게임을 좋다. **(Incorrect)**
  The adjective 좋다 cannot be used after the object "게임을."

The adjective 좋다 can be used only with first person subject

In the *subject A + subject B + adjective (좋다)* structure, subject A must be first person. This is because the adjective 좋다 is a psychological adjective to describe the personal feeling of a first person subject.

- 나는 꽃이 좋다. **(Correct)** *(I **like** flowers.)*
  너는 꽃이 좋다. **(Incorrect)**
  The adjective 좋다 cannot be used with the second person subject "너는."

- 우리는 공부가 **좋다**. **(Correct)** *(We like studying.)*
  내 누나는 공부가 **좋다**. **(Incorrect)**
  The adjective 좋다 cannot be used with the third person subject "내 누나는."

The Verb 좋아하다

Listen to Track 123

The verb **좋아하다** is easy to use, since it is a verb and it means *"to like."* Let's look at some examples of how we can use it and when we cannot use it.

How to use the verb 좋아하다

As **좋아하다** is a verb, you can use it after objects, which are indicated with the object particle -를/-을.

- 을 is used when the preceding syllable ends with a consonant.
- 를 is used when the preceding syllable ends with a vowel.

Remember:	Korean follows the Subject + Object + Verb structure.

- 나는 너를 **좋아한다**. *(I **like** you.)*
  You can use the verb 좋아한다 after the object "너를."

- 내 형은 승마를 **좋아한다**. *(My brother **likes** horse riding.)*
  You can use the verb 좋아한다 after the object "승마를."

- 내 부모님은 여행을 **좋아한다**. *(My parents **like** traveling.)*
  You can use the verb 좋아한다 after the object "여행을."

When you cannot use the verb 좋아하다

The verb **좋아하다** can only be after objects.

Since the verb 좋아하다 is a transitive verb, it cannot be used after subjects. It needs to follow the *subject + object + verb* structure.

Listen to Track 124

- 나는 네가 **좋다**. **(Correct)** *(I **like** you.)*
  나는 네**가 좋아한다**. **(Incorrect)**
  There is no object for the transitive verb 좋아하다.

- 나는 수학이 **좋다**. **(Correct)** *(I **like** Mathematics.)*
  나는 수학이 좋**아한다**. **(Incorrect)**
  There is no object for the transitive verb 좋아하다.

The verb 좋아하다 means "you like it because you experienced it before"

The verb 좋아하다 sounds weird when you use it to describe first experience. You should use the adjective 좋다 instead in this case. Although both the adjective 좋다 and the verb 좋아하다 mean the verb "to like," 좋아하다 specifically means a preference for something you have experienced before.

Listen to Track 125

- **(Seeing a new toy for the first time)** 이 장난감이 **좋아요**. **(Correct)**
  *(I **like** this new toy.)*
  (Seeing a new toy for the first time) 이 장난감을 **좋아해요**. **(Incorrect)**
  좋아하다 sounds weird because you never played with the new toy before.
  (After playing with a toy for a while) 이 장난감을 **좋아해요**. **(Correct)**
  *(I **like** this toy.)*

- **(Right after a blind date)** 나는 이 남자가 **좋아**. **(Correct)**
  *(I **like** this man.)* [whom I never met before]
  (Right after a blind date) 나는 이 남자를 **좋아한다**. **(Incorrect)**
  It is possible to fall in love at first sight. 좋아하다 sounds weird, however, as you have never met him before.
  (After being a couple for a while) 나는 이 남자를 **좋아한다**. **(Correct)**
  *(I **like** this man.)* [whom I have been going out with]

TIME TO PRACTICE!

Sentence Structure and 좋다 vs. 좋아하다

Exercise 1: Choose the right word in the following sentences:

1. 그는 성격이 [좋다 / 좋아한다]. *(His personality is good.)* _____
2. 내 고양이는 참치를 [좋다 / 좋아한다]. *(My cat likes tuna.)* _____
3. 나는 와인보다는 맥주를 [좋다 / 좋아한다]. *(I prefer beer to wine.)* _____
4. 그가 일하는 태도는 굉장히 [좋다 / 좋아한다]. *(His work attitude is really good.)* _____
5. 현재 그녀는 건강이 매우 [좋다 / 좋아한다]. *(She is very healthy now.)* _____
6. 나는 그녀가 [좋다 / 좋아한다]. *(I like her.)* _____
7. 나는 친구들과 농구하는 것을 [좋다 / 좋아한다]. *(I like playing basketball with my friends.)* _____
8. 내 형은 매일 운동을 해서 몸이 [좋다 / 좋아한다]. *(My brother is in good shape as he works out every day.)* _____
9. 나는 그녀를 [좋다 / 좋아한다]. *(I like her.)* _____
10. 오늘은 날씨가 [좋다 / 좋아한다]. *(Today's weather is good.)* _____

Exercise 2: Determine if the following sentences are Correct / Incorrect:

1. 나는 맛있는 음식을 먹어서 기분이 좋아한다. *(I feel good because I ate delicious food).* _____
2. 이 집은 우리 가족이 살기 좋다. *(This house is good to live in for my family.)* _____
3. 나는 친구들과 사이가 좋다. *(I get along with my friends well.)* _____
4. 내 동생은 그림 실력이 좋아한다. *(My sister's drawing skills are good.)* _____
5. 나는 클래식 음악이 좋다. *(I like classical music.)* _____
6. 내 누나는 장미를 좋다. *(My sister likes roses.)* _____
7. 나는 스위스 음식이 좋아한다. *(I like Swiss food.)* _____
8. 내 강아지는 산책을 좋아한다. *(My dog likes taking a walk.)* _____
9. 내 강아지와 고양이는 서로 사이가 좋다. *(My dog and cat get along well.)* _____
10. 내 친구들은 축구를 좋아한다. *(My friends like soccer.)* _____

Exercise 3: Determine if the following statements are True / False:

1. Although 좋다 is an adjective, it can be used after an object. _____
2. When 좋다 means "to like," double subjects are not needed. _____
3. 좋다 can be used with a first-person subject. _____
4. Both 좋다 and 좋아하다 can be used with a third person subject. _____
5. 좋아하다 cannot be used with a second person subject. _____
6. 좋아하다 can be used after a subject. _____
7. In sentences with double subjects, both subjects work as subjects. _____
8. 좋다 becomes a verb when it means "to like." _____
9. Both English and Korean have the "S + V + O" structure. _____
10. It is possible to make a sentence without a verb in Korean. _____

Exercise 4: Choose the meaning of 좋다 in the following sentences:

1. 내 동생은 성격이 좋다. [Good / To like]   성격: *personality*
2. 나는 내 고양이가 좋다. [Good / To like]   고양이: *cat*
3. 이 컴퓨터는 성능이 좋다. [Good / To like]   컴퓨터: *computer*
                                                   성능: *performance*
4. 나는 프랑스 음식이 좋다. [Good / To like]   프랑스: *France*
5. 프랑스 음식은 모양이 좋다. [Good / To like]   모양: *shape / look*
6. 나는 레이싱 게임이 좋다. [Good / To like]   레이싱: *racing,* 게임: *video game*
7. 나는 빨간색이 좋다. [Good / To like]   빨간색: *red*
8. 빨간색은 주의를 끌기에 좋다. [Good / To like]   주의: *attention*
9. 녹차는 몸에 좋다. [Good / To like]   녹차: *green tea*
10. 나는 블루베리가 좋다. [Good / To like]   블루베리: *blueberry*

Exercise 5: Fill in the blanks with 좋다 / 좋아한다 to complete the following sentences:

1. 나는 고양이와 강아지가 둘 다 _____. (*I like both cats and dogs.*)
2. 나는 수학을 _____. (*I like mathematics.*)
3. 나는 한국 음식을 _____. (*I like Korean food.*)
4. 내 고양이는 낮잠 자는 것을 _____. (*My cat likes taking a nap.*)
5. 내 핸드폰은 화질이 _____. (*My phone's display is good.*)
6. 나는 체코 음식이 _____. (*I like Czech food.*)
7. 나는 부모님과 소풍가는 것이 _____. (*I like going on a picnic with my parents.*)

8. 내 동생은 자전거 타는 것을 _____. *(My brother likes riding a bicycle.)*
9. 나는 한국어 공부하는 것을 _____. *(I like studying Korean.)*
10. 이 꽃의 향기가 _____. *(This flower smells good.)*

ANSWERS:

Exercise 1

1. 좋다 / 2. 좋아한다 / 3. 좋아한다. / 4. 좋다 / 5. 좋다 / 6. 좋다 / 7. 좋아한다 /
8. 좋다 / 9. 좋아한다 / 10. 좋다

Exercise 2

1. Incorrect (좋아한다 -> 좋다) / 2. Correct / 3. Correct / 4. Incorrect
(좋아한다 -> 좋다) / 5. Correct / 6. Incorrect (좋다 -> 좋아한다) / 7. Incorrect
(음식이 -> 음식을) / 8. Correct / 9. Correct / 10. Correct

Exercise 3

1. False (It cannot be used after an object.) / 2. False (Double subjects are
needed.) / 3. True / 4. True / 5. False (It can be used with a second person
subject.) / 6. False (It can be used after an object.) / 7. False (In sentences
with double subjects, one subject works as a subject and the other works as an
adverb.) / 8. True / 9. False (Korean has S+O+V structure.) / 10. True

Exercise 4

1. Good (My brother's personality is good.) / 2. To like (I like my cat.) /
3. Good (The performance of this computer is good.) / 4. To like (I like
French food.) / 5. Good (French food looks good.) / 6. To like (I like racing
games.) / 7. To like (I like red.) / Good (Red is good to draw attention.) /
9. Good (Green tea is good for health.) / 10. To like (I like blueberries.)

Exercise 5

1. 좋다 / 2. 좋아한다 / 3. 좋아한다 / 4. 좋아한다 / 5. 좋다 / 6. 좋다 / 7. 좋다 /
8. 좋아한다 / 9. 좋아한다 / 10. 좋다

QUICK RECAP

Today you learned about the adjective 좋다 and the verb 좋아하다. You also learned about the differences between the two words and the new Korean sentence structure *Subject A + Subject B + Adjective (좋다).*

It can be tricky to use this unique Korean sentence structure. It is totally rewarding, however, as your writing will look more native and your speech will sound more natural. You did an excellent job today!

	The Adjective 좋다	**The Verb 좋아하다.**
After	A subject	An object
Using	1: Subject + adjective (좋다) 2: Subject A + subject B + adjective (좋다)	Subject + Object + Verb (좋아하다)
With	A first person subject	A first / second / third person subject
Meaning	1: Subject is good. 2: Subject A likes subject B.	Subject likes object
For	General preferences	Preferences based on past experiences

LESSON 13: QUALIFIERS IN KOREAN

In this lesson, we will learn about the Korean qualifiers and quantifiers. **Qualifiers** are the words used to attribute quality to other words. For example, English words such as "very," "really," "not really," and "not at all" are qualifiers.

In Korean, some adverbs work as qualifiers. There are six Korean qualifiers: **아주, 정말, 진짜, 조금, 별로, 전혀**. Let us learn the meanings of these words, and see how we can use them in sentences.

How to Use Korean Adverbs and Adjectives

The grammar in this lesson is simple. The one thing we have to know today is how to use Korean adverbs and adjectives. This time, we are lucky! Korean adverbs and adjectives work in the same way as English adverbs and adjectives do; the adverbs modify adjectives, verbs, or other adverbs, and the adjectives modify nouns in both languages.

As the Korean qualifiers do not change the forms of adjectives, we can simply add these words without spending time to find the infinitives of adjectives. Let us look at where we can put them in sentences.

1) 아주

**Listen to Track 126**

Meaning the adverbs "very (much)," "so," "extremely," "exceedingly"

The adverb 아주 modifies an adjective, a verb, or an adverb. You can put it before the adjective, verb, or adverb that it will modify.

- 공기가 **아주 건조하다**. (_The air is **exceedingly dry.**_)
  The adverb 아주 modifies the adjective "건조하다 (dry)," adding the meaning of "exceedingly."

- 어제는 **아주 더웠다**. (*It was **extremely hot** yesterday.*)

  The adverb 아주 modifies the adjective "덥다 (hot)," adding the meaning of "extremely."

- **아주 즐거웠다**. (*I was **very pleased**.*)

  The adverb 아주 modifies the adjective "즐겁다 (pleased)," adding the meaning of "very."

- 시험이 **아주 쉬웠다**. (*The exam was **so easy**.*)

  The adverb 아주 modifies the adjective "쉽다 (easy)," adding the meaning of "so."

- **아주 오래전에** 그를 만났다. (*I met him **a very long time ago.**)*

  The adverb 아주 modifies the adverb "오래전에 (a long time ago)," adding the meaning of "very."

Meaning "completely," "totally"

Listen to Track 127

- 이 보고서는 **아주 정확하다**. (*This report is **completely accurate**.*)

  The adverb 아주 modifies the adverb "정확하다 (accurate)," adding the meaning of "completely."

- 그의 작품은 **아주 완벽하다**. (*His masterpiece is **totally perfect**.*)

  The adverb 아주 modifies the adverb "완벽하다 (perfect)," adding the meaning of "totally."

2) 정말

Listen to Track 128

The adverb 정말 modifies an adjective, a verb, or an adverb. You can put it before the adjective, verb, or adverb that it will modify.

Meaning the adverbs "truly," "really," "indeed"

- **정말 미안합니다**. (*I am **truly sorry**.*)

  The adverb 정말 modifies the adjective "미안하다 (sorry)," adding the meaning of "truly."

- **정말 뜻밖의** 결과다. *(The result is **really unexpected**.)*

  The adverb 정말 modifies the adjective "뜻밖이다 (unexpected)," adding the meaning of "really."

- 그는 **정말 똑똑하다**. *(He is **really smart**.)*

  The adverb 정말 modifies the adjective "똑똑하다 (smart)," adding the meaning of "really."

- **정말** 영광입니다. *(It is **indeed** an honor to meet you.)*

  The adverb 정말 adds the meaning of "indeed."

- **정말 잘했어요**! *(You did a **really good job**!)*

  The adverb 정말 modifies the verb "잘하다 (do good)," adding the meaning of "really."

3) 진짜

Listen to Track 129

The adverb 진짜 modifies an adjective, a verb, or an adverb. You can put it before the adjective, verb, or adverb that it will modify. 진짜 can also be an adjective. When it is used as an adjective, it modifies a noun after it.

Meaning the adverbs "really," "very," "truly," "indeed"

- 이 영화는 **진짜 지루하다**. *(This movie is **very boring**.)*

  The adverb 진짜 modifies the adjective "지루하다 (boring)," adding the meaning of "very."

- 그는 **진짜 대단하다**. *(He is **truly amazing**.)*

  The adverb 진짜 modifies the adjective "대단하다 (amazing)," adding the meaning of "truly."

- 그는 **진짜 화났다**. *(He is **really angry**.)*

  The adverb 진짜 modifies the adjective "화나다 (angry)," adding the meaning of "really."

Meaning the adjective "real"

Listen To Track 130

- 그녀는 **진짜 천재다**. (*She is a **real genius**.*)
  The adjective 진짜 modifies the noun "천재 (genius)," adding the meaning of "real."

- 이 사진은 **진짜 사진이** 아니다. (*This photo is not a **real photo**.*)
  The adjective 진짜 modifies the noun "사진 (photo)," adding the meaning of "real."

- 그는 **진짜 전문가다**. (*He is a **real expert**.*)
  The adjective 진짜 modifies the noun "전문가 (expert)," adding the meaning of "real."

> *The adverbs 아주, 정말, and 진짜 have the same meaning. The difference between them is that 아주 is a pure Korean word (first recorded in 1576) while the other two are words from the Chinese characters 정 (正, "right") and 진 (眞, "true").*

4) 조금

Listen to Track 131

The adverb 조금 modifies an adjective, a verb, or an adverb. You can put it before the adjective, verb, or adverb that it will modify.

Meaning "some," "a little," "a bit," "a while," "(for) a moment"

- 오늘은 **조금 피곤하다**. (*I am **a little bit tired** today.*)
  The adverb 조금 modifies the adjective "피곤하다 (tired)," adding the meaning of "a little bit."

- 한국어를 **조금 할 수 있어요**. (*I can speak Korean **a little bit**.*)
  The adverb 조금 modifies the verb "하다 (do [Korean] -> speak)," adding the meaning of "a little bit."

- 제 의견은 **조금 다릅니다**. (*My opinions **differ a little**.*)

The adverb 조금 modifies the verb "다르다 (differ)," adding the meaning of "a little."

- **조금** 뒤에 다시 **전화해주세요**. *(Please **call back a little** later.)*
  The adverb 조금 modifies "뒤에(later)" adding the meaning of "a little later."

- 우리는 **조금 늦을** 것 같다. *(We will be **a bit late**.)*
  The adverb 조금 modifies the verb "늦다 (late)," adding the meaning of "a bit." (The word "late" is a verb in Korean.)

5) 별로

Listen to Track 132

The adverb 별로 modifies an adjective, a verb, or an adverb. You can put it before the adjective, verb, or adverb that it will modify. Since the adverb 별로 has a negative meaning, you can use it only in negative sentences.

Meaning "(not) especially," "(not) particularly," "(not) really"

- **별로** 할 일이 **없다**. **(Correct)** *(I do not have anything to do in particular.)*
  The adverb 별로 adds the meaning of "(not) in particular."

- 이 게임은 **별로** 재미있지 **않다**. **(Correct)** *(This game is **not really** fun.)*
  The adverb 별로 adds the meaning of "(not) really."

  나는 **별로** 행복하다. **(Incorrect)** *(I am especially happy.)*
  As the adverb 별로 has a negative meaning, it can be used only in negative sentences.

6) 전혀

Listen to Track 133

The adverb 전혀 modifies an adjective, a verb, or an adverb. You can put it before the adjective, verb, or adverb that it will modify. It can be used in negative sentences, or with adjectives implying negative meaning: such as "다르다 (different, not the same)," and "예기치 못하다 (unexpected)."

Meaning "(not) at all," "(not) in the least," "completely," "absolutely," "entirely"

- 나는 그 일에 **전혀** 관심이 **없다**. **(Correct)** *(I am not in the least interested in that.)*

  The adverb 전혀 adds the meaning of "(not) in the least"

  나는 그 일에 **전혀** 관심이 있다. **(Incorrect)** *(I am interested in that.)*

  As the sentence is not negative and no adjectives are implying negative meaning, the adverb 전혀 cannot be used.

- 그는 **전혀 다른** 사람 같았다. *(He seemed a **completely different** person.)*

  Used with the adjective "different" which implies the negative meaning "not the same," the adverb adds the meaning of "completely."

TIME TO PRACTICE!

Qualifiers in Korean

Exercise 1. Choose the right position to put 아주, 정말, or 진짜.

1. ① 공기가 ② 건조하다 ③. *(The air is really dry.)* _____
2. ① 어제는 ② 추웠다 ③. *(It was so cold yesterday.)* _____
3. ① 오늘 ② 재미있었다 ③. *(It was really fun today.)* _____
4. ① 시험이 ② 어려웠다 ③. *(The exam was extremely difficult.)* _____
5. ① 나는 ② 오래전에 ③ 그녀를 ④ 만났다 ⑤. *(I met her a very long time ago.)* _____
6. ① 이 ② 그림은 ③ 아름답다 ④. *(This picture is really beautiful.)* _____
7. ① 그녀는 ② 똑똑하다 ③. *(She is really smart.)* _____
8. ① 만나게 ② 되어 ③ 영광입니다 ④. *(It is indeed an honor to meet you.)* _____
9. ① 이 ② 게임은 ③ 지루하다 ④. *(This video game is really boring.)* _____
10. ① 내 ② 고양이는 ③ 귀엽다 ④. *(My cat is so cute.)* _____

Exercise 2. Choose the right one in the following sentences:

1. 오늘은 [조금 / 별로 / 전혀] 졸리다. *(I am a little bit sleepy today.)* _____
2. 저는 체코어를 [조금 / 별로 / 전혀] 할 수 있어요. *(I can speak Czech little bit.)*
3. 이 컴퓨터는 [조금 / 별로 / 전혀] 비싸다. *(This computer is a little bit expensive.)* _____
4. 이 책은 [조금 / 별로 / 전혀] 재미 없다. *(This book is not really interesting.)* _____
5. 나는 [조금 / 별로 / 전혀] 배고프지 않다. *(I am not hungry at all.)* _____
6. 나는 그를 [조금 / 별로 / 전혀] 보고싶지 않다. *(I do not miss him at all.)* _____
7. [조금 / 별로 / 전혀] 뒤에 다시 메일 보내주세요. *(Please resend the email a little later.)* _____
8. 나는 [조금 / 별로 / 전혀] 배고프지 않다. *(I am not really hungry.)* _____
9. 나는 [조금 / 별로 / 전혀] 배고프다. *(I am a little bit hungry.)* _____
10. 내 고양이는 [조금 / 별로 / 전혀] 피곤해보인다. *(My cat looks a little bit tired.)* _____

Exercise 3. Fill in the blank in the following sentences:

1. 이 휴대폰은 _____ 비싸지 않다. *(This phone is not really expensive.)*
2. 이 영화는 _____ 재미 없다. *(This movie is not fun at all.)*
3. 나는 _____ 아프다. *(I am little bit sick.)*
4. 나는 _____ 차이를 못 느끼겠다. *(I do not really see a big difference.)*
5. 나는 오늘 _____ 할 일이 없다. *(I do not have anything to do in particular.)*
6. 그녀는 _____ 다른 사람 같았다. *(She seemed a completely different person.)*
7. 나는 낮잠을 _____ 잤다. *(I took a nap a little bit. / I took a little nap.)*
8. 나는 _____ 관심 없다. *(I am not really interested.)*
9. 나는 _____ 귀여운 강아지를 봤다. *(I saw a very cute puppy.)*
10. 나는 오늘 기분이 _____ 좋다. *(I feel so good today.)*

Exercise 4. Determine if the following sentences are Correct / Incorrect:

1. 나는 별로 행복하다. *(I am not really happy.)* _____
2. 나는 테니스를 전혀 좋아한다. *(I really like playing tennis.)* _____
3. 그 영화배우는 정말 멋지다. *(That actress is really cool.)* _____
4. 오늘 별로 습했다. *(It was so humid today.)* _____
5. 친구와 축구하는 것은 아주 재미있다. *(Playing soccer with friends is really fun.)* _____
6. 나는 오늘 아주 피곤하다. *(I feel so tired today.)* _____
7. 내 동생은 정말 똑똑하다. *(My sister is really smart.)* _____
8. 시험은 전혀 어렵지 않았다. *(The exam was not difficult at all.)* _____
9. 이 차는 전혀 비싸다. *(This car is really expensive.)* _____
10. 나는 별로 배고프지 않다. *(I am not really hungry.)* _____

Exercise 5. Check if the following statements are True / False:

1. 아주, 정말, 진짜 cannot be used interchangeably. _____
2. 별로 can only be used in a negative sentence. _____
3. 전혀 cannot be used in a negative sentence. _____
4. 진짜 can mean the adjective "real" in English. _____
5. 아주 and 정말 are adverbs. _____
6. Korean qualifiers change the form of an adjective. _____
7. You have to find an infinitive of a verb to use 진짜. _____
8. You can use a Korean adverb before an adjective. _____
9. 별로 implies a negative meaning. _____
10. 전혀 can be used with an adjective that implies negative meaning. _____

ANSWERS:

Exercise 1

1. ② / 2. ② / 3. ② / 4. ② / 5. ② / 6. ③ / 7. ② / 8. ③ / 9. ③ / 10. ③

Exercise 2

1. 조금 / 2. 조금 / 3. 조금 / 4. 별로 / 5. 전혀 / 6. 전혀 / 7. 조금 / 8. 별로 / 9. 조금 / 10. 조금

Exercise 3

1. 별로 / 2. 전혀 / 3. 조금 / 4. 별로 / 5. 별로 / 6. 전혀 / 7. 조금 / 8. 별로 / 9. 아주 (정말, 진짜) / 10. 아주 (정말, 진짜)

Exercise 4

1. Incorrect (행복하다 -> 행복하지 않다) / 2. Incorrect (전혀 –> 아주/정말/진짜) / 3. Correct / 4. Incorrect (별로 -> 아주/정말/진짜) / 5. Correct / 6. Correct / 7. Correct / 8. Correct / 9. Incorrect (전혀 -> 아주/정말/진짜) / 10. Correct

Exercise 5

1. False (They can be used interchangeably.) / 2. True / 3. False (It can be used in a negative sentence.) / 4. True / 5. True / 6. False (It does not change the form of an adjective.) / 7. False (You don't have to find an infinitive to use 진짜.) / 8. True / 9. True / 10. True

QUICK RECAP

Today, you learned about the Korean qualifiers. Qualifiers are common components in Korean, and knowing how to use them correctly will definitely make your writing and speaking appear more natural. You did a good job today!

	아주	정말	진짜	조금	별로	전혀
Meaning	Very / Really / Totally / Truly			A little bit	Not really	Not at all
For	Plain Sentence				Negative Sentence	
Part of Speech	Adverb		Adverb Adjective	Adverb		

LESSON 14: THE MOST USEFUL ADVERBS

As you are aware, an adverb is a word that modifies an adjective, a verb, or another adverb to give emphasis or provide a greater description.

There are countless Korean adverbs you will add to your vocabulary in time; but for now, we have some of the most useful adverbs to give you a running start. These adverbs are divided into five different categories telling how they are used to help you learn them more easily.

Listen to Track 134

1. To give emphasis

Positive emphasis

- 너무 *(too)*
- 아주 *(very)*
- 정말 *(really/truly)*

Example sentences:

You can use any of the above three words to emphasize that something is delicious:

- **너무** 맛있어요. *(It tastes **too** good.)*
- **아주** 맛있어요. *(It tastes **very** good.)*
- **정말** 맛있어요. *(It tastes **really** good.)*

Let's look at a few more sentences:

Listen to Track 135

- 그 공원이 **너무** 멀어요. *(That park is **too** far from here.)*
- 우리 아들이 한국음식을 **아주** 좋아해요. *(Our son likes Korean food **very** much.)*
- 저는 **정말** 몰랐어요. *(I **really** didn't know.)*

> **Note:** *The word "정말" can also be used as a noun/adjective. 정말이에요. [That] is the truth. / [What I'm saying] is true. 정말이에요? Is [that] the truth? / Is [that] true?*

Negative emphasis

The following three adverbs are used only when making a negative statement. It is important to note that although the adverbs already indicate the negative, they must be used along with the negative form of the verb.

Listen to Track 136

- 절대 [절때] *(never)*
- 전혀 *(not at all)*
- 별로 *(not very much / not very good)*

Example sentences:

As you look at each sentence, notice that the verbs are in their negative form.

Listen to Track 137

Sentence	Translation	Verb used
그 사람을 **절대** 용서 안 할 거예요.	*I will never forgive that person.*	하다 *(to do)* 할 거예요 *(will do)* **안 할 거예요** *(will not do)*
그 집은 **절대** 팔지 마세요.	*Please don't ever sell that house.*	팔다 *(to sell)* 파세요 *(please sell)* **팔지 마세요** *(please do not sell)*
저는 한식을 **전혀** 안 좋아해요.	*I do not like Korean food at all.*	좋아하다 *(to like)* 좋아해요 *(do like)* **안 좋아해요** *(do not like)*
저는 요리를 **전혀** 못해요.	*I cannot cook at all.*	하다 *(to do)* 해요 *(do)* **못 해요** *(cannot do)*

이 피자집은 **별로** 맛이 없어요.	*This pizza place does not taste very good.*	맛이 없다 *(to not taste good)* **맛이 없어요** *(does not taste good)*
저는 과자를 **별로** 안 좋아해요.	*I do not like cookies very much.*	좋아하다 *(to like)* 좋아해요 *(do like)* **안 좋아해요** *(do not like)*

2. To indicate speed & distance

Listen to Track 138

We will look at four common adverbs for describing speed and distance:

- 빨리 *(quickly)*
- 천천히 [천처니] *(slowly)*
- 멀리 *(far away)*
- 가까이 *(close by)*

Listen to Track 139

Sentence	Translation
이 작업을 **빨리** 끝내야 해요.	*I have to finish this job **quickly**.*
시간이 많으니까 **천천히** 갑시다.	*Since we have a lot of time, let's go **slowly**.*
저는 어디 **멀리** 여행을 가고 싶어요.	*I want to travel somewhere **far away**.*
우리는 **가까이** 살아서 자주 만날 수 있어요.	*Since we live **close by**, we can get together often.*

Note: *The word "가까이" can also indicate closeness in relationships: 우리 나이가 비슷하니까 가까이 지냅시다. Since we are similar in age, let's be **closer** friends.*

3. In relation to people

Listen to Track 140

Below are three common adverbs generally used in relation to people:

- 같이 [가치] *(together / like [similar to])*
- 함께 *(together)*
- 서로 *(each other)*

The first two adverbs 같이 and 함께 have the same meaning and can be used interchangeably. However, the word 같이 also has a second meaning to indicate "like" or "similar to" something/someone else.

Example sentences:

Listen to Track 141

Sentence	Translation
엄마하고 아빠가 **같이** 오실 거예요.	*Mom and dad will be coming **together**.*
그 사람과 **같이** 행동하면 안 돼요.	*You shouldn't act **like** that person.*
그 여자의 목소리가 남자**같이** 굵어요.	*That woman's voice is deep **like** a man's.*
우리 식구는 매일 **함께** 저녁을 먹어요.	*Our family eats dinner **together** every day.*
그들이 **함께** 싸웠어요.	*They fought **together**.*
두 사람은 **서로** 오해하고 있어요.	*The two people are misunderstanding **each other**.*
우리는 **서로** 안 맞는 성격이에요.	*We have incompatible personalities with **each other**.*

4. To indicate how and to what degree

In this category, we will be looking at some more common adverbs and an example sentence for each:

Listen to Track 142

Adverb	Translation	Example sentence
많이	a lot / many	어제 파티에 사람들이 **많이** 왔어요. ***Many*** *people came to the party yesterday.*
적당히	just enough	마이클이 건강을 유지하기 위해 운동을 **적당히** 하는 것 같아요. *I think Michael exercises **just enough** to stay fit.*
조용히	quietly	도서관에서 **조용히** 말해야 돼요. *[You] have to speak quietly at the library.*
대단히	greatly	오늘 **대단히** 즐거웠어요. *[I] **greatly** enjoyed my time today.*
완전히	completely	숙제를 보고 **완전히** 끝내세요. *Look over the homework and finish it **completely**.*
확실히	certainly	한국어는 **확실히** 어려운 언어예요. *Korean is **certainly** a hard language.*
충분히	thoroughly	나중에 **충분히** 설명해 줄게요. *I will explain it to you **thoroughly** later.*

5. To indicate time and frequency

Listed below are 12 common adverbs of time and frequency, along with an example sentence for each:

Listen to Track 143

Adverb	Translation	Example sentence
다시	again	우리 언제 **다시** 만나요? *When will we meet **again**?*

먼저	before/ahead	제가 **먼저** 도착했어요. *I arrived **ahead** [of you or someone].*
미리	ahead of time	그 식당에 **미리** 예약 해놨어요. *[I] made a reservation **ahead of time** at the restaurant.*
벌써	already	왜 **벌써** 가세요? *Why are [you] leaving **already**?*
이미	already (past)	그 사람은 **이미** 왔다 갔어요. *That person **already** came and went.*
아직	not yet / still	**아직** 준비가 안 됐어요. *[I] am **not yet** ready. (This adverb is used with negative sentences containing "not.")*
자꾸	repeatedly	단어를 **자꾸** 잊어버려요. *[I] **repeatedly** forget the word.*
항상	always	저는 갈 준비가 **항상** 돼 있어요. *I am **always** ready to go.*
가끔	occasionally	학생들이 **가끔** 지각을 해요. *The students are **occasionally** tardy.*
자주	frequently / often	우리 집에 **자주** 놀러 오세요. *Please visit our house **often**.*
계속	continuously	이번 주에 **계속** 비가 와요. *It rains (is raining) **continuously** this week.*
일찍	early	오늘 아침에 **일찍** 일어났어요. *[I] got up **early** this morning.*

Two or more adverbs used together

Just as it is true in English sentences, Korean sentences can also contain two or more adverbs together. Here are some examples:

Listen to Track 144

Sentence	Translation	Adverbs used
우리 **다 같이** 가요.	*Let's **all** go **together**.*	다 (*all*); 같이 (*together*)

물 **좀 더** 주세요.	*Please give me **some more** water.*	좀 (*some*); 더 (*more*)
다음에는 **좀 덜** 맵게 만들어 주세요.	*Next time, please make it **somewhat less** spicy.*	좀 (*somewhat*); 덜 (*less*); 맵게 (*spicy*)
눈이 **너무 많이** 와요.	*It snows **too much**.*	너무 (*too*); 많이 (*a lot/much*)
제 실력이 **아직 많이** 부족해요.	*My skills are **still very much** lacking.*	아직 (*still*); 많이 (*a lot/much*)
내일은 **좀 더** 일찍 올 수 있어요?	*Can you come **somewhat more early** (earlier) tomorrow?*	좀 (*somewhat*); 더 (*more*); 일찍 (*early*)

TIME TO PRACTICE!

The Most Useful Adverbs

Exercise 1. Find the adverbs in the following sentences:

1. 저는 오늘 아주 기분이 좋아요. *(I feel really good today.)* -> Adverb: _____

2. 이 영화는 전혀 재미 있지 않아요. *(This movie is not interesting at all.)* -> Adverb: _____

3. 저는 가끔 영웅이 되는 상상을 해요. -> Adverb: _____ *(I sometimes dream of being a hero.)*

4. 별로 기분이 좋지 않아요. *(I don't really feel well.)* -> Adverb: _____

5. 저는 점심을 너무 많이 먹었어요. *(I had too much lunch.)* -> Adverb: _____

6. 천천히 숨을 쉬세요. *(Please breathe slowly.)* -> Adverb: _____

7. 티켓을 모두 다 모았나요? *(Did you collect all your tickets?)* -> Adverb: _____

8. 기차가 다리 위를 빨리 달리고 있어요. -> Adverb: _____ *(The train is running fast on the bridge.)*

9. 멀리서 경찰이 오고 있어요. -> Adverb: _____ 멀리 *(The police are coming from a distance.)*

10. 우리 함께 저녁 먹으러 가자. *(Let's go eat dinner together.)* -> Adverb: _____ 함께

Exercise 2. Fi ll in the blanks with the correct adverbs to complete the sentences:

1. 내 고양이는 _____ 귀엽다. *(My cat is so cute.)*

2. _____ 운동을 하는 것이 좋다. *(Working out appropriately is good for your health.)*

3. _____ 도전하라. 절대 포기하지 마라. *(Keep trying. Never give up.)*

4. 그 뉴스가 _____ 사실이야? *(Is that news really true?)*

5. _____ 설명해 주세요. *(Please explain it to me thoroughly.)*

6. 나는 _____ 그를 배신하지 않을 것이다. *(I will never betray him.)*

7. 레오나르도 디카프리오는 _____ 좋은 배우예요. *(Leonardo DiCaprio is certainly a good actor.)*

8. 조금 더 _____ 오세요. (*Please come a little closer.*)

9. 수업이 _____ 끝날 때까지 기다려주세요. (*Please wait until the lesson is completely finished.*)

10. 두 사람은 _____ 오해하고 있어요. (*They are misunderstanding each other.*)

Exercise 3. Choose the correct adverbs to complete the following sentences:

1. 그가 그런 짓을 했다는 것은 [아주 / 전혀] 이상하지 않다. (*It is not strange at all that he did that.*) _____

2. 나는 [별로 / 전혀] 배 안 고파. (*I am not really hungry.*) _____

3. [더 / 덜] 노력해라. (*Try harder.*) _____

4. 너무 [조금 / 많이] 먹는 것은 건강에 좋지 않다. (*Overeating is not good for your health.*)_____

5. 너무 [천천히 / 빨리] 가지마. (*Don't go too fast.*) _____

6. 나는 [항상 / 가끔] 그와 행복했던 추억을 생각한다. (*I sometimes think of happy memories with him.*) _____

7. [이미 / 아직] 비행기가 출발했다. (*The plane has already departed.*) _____

8. 나는 종이 비행기를 [멀리 / 가까이] 던졌다. (*I threw a paper plane far away.*) _____

9. 관세가 [일찍 / 다시] 높아질 예정이다. (*It is expected that tariffs will rise again.*) _____

10. [자꾸 / 먼저] 출발해라. (*Start first.*) _____

Exercise 4. Determine if the following sentences are Correct / Incorrect:

1. 나는 액션 영화를 별로 좋아한다. (*I like action movies very much.*)_____

2. 이 음식은 너무 맛있다. (*This food is really delicious.*) _____

3. 저는 스위스 음식을 정말 좋아해요. (*I really like Swiss food.*) _____

4. 저는 그녀를 절대 용서할 거에요. (*I will never forgive her.*) _____

5. 저는 골프를 전혀 못 쳐요. (*I cannot play golf at all.*) _____

6. 말들이 천천히 달리고 있다. (*Horses are running fast.*) _____

7. 벌써 일을 끝냈어요? (*Did you finish your work already?*) _____

8. 이 반찬 좀 덜 주세요. (*Please give me more of this side dish.*) _____

9. 나는 가끔 일찍 일어난다. (*I always wake up early.*) _____

10. 이미 축제는 끝났다. (*The festival is already over.*) _____

ANSWERS:

Exercise 1

1. 아주 / 2. 전혀 / 3. 가끔 / 4. 별로 / 5. 너무 / 6. 천천히 / 7. 다 / 8. 빨리 / 9. 멀리 / 10. 함께

Exercise 2

1. 너무 / 2. 적당히 / 3. 계속 / 4. 정말 / 5. 충분히 / 6. 절대 / 7. 확실히 / 8. 가까이 / 9. 완전히 / 10. 서로

Exercise 3

1. 전혀 / 2. 별로 / 3. 더 / 4. 많이 / 5. 빨리 / 6. 가끔 / 7. 이미 / 8. 멀리 / 9. 다시 / 10. 먼저

Exercise 4

1. Incorrect: 별로 -> 아주 / 매우 / 정말 / 2. Correct / 3. Correct / 4. Incorrect: "절대" should be used with a negative verb (용서 할 거에요 -> 용서하지 않을 거에요). / 5. Correct / 6. Incorrect: 천천히 (slowly) -> 빨리 (fast) / 7. Correct / 8. Incorrect: 덜 (less) -> 더 (more) / 9. Incorrect: 가끔 (sometimes) -> 항상 (always) / 10. Correct

QUICK RECAP

In this lesson, we have learned various useful adverbs that are commonly used in the Korean language. To help you review the words, the adverbs from this lesson are in a comprehensive list below. We encourage you to continue to practice using them in various Korean sentences.

Listen to Track 145

Emphasis	Speed/ distance	People- related	How/ To What Degree	Time & frequency
너무 (too)	빨리 (quickly)	같이 (together/like)	조용히 (quietly)	다시 (again)
아주 (very)	천천히 (slowly)	함께 (together)	대단히 (greatly)	먼저 (before/ahead)
정말 (really/truly)	멀리 (far away)	서로 (with each other)	확실히 (certainly)	미리 (ahead of time)
절대 (never)	가까이 (close by)		완전히 (completely)	벌써 (already)
전혀 (not at all)			조금 (a little bit)	이미 (already - past)
별로 (not much)			많이 (a lot/much)	아직 (not yet/still)
			적당히 (just enough)	자꾸 (repeatedly)
			충분히 (thoroughly)	항상 (always)
				가끔 (occasionally)
				자주 (frequently / often)
				계속 (continuously)
				일찍 (early)

147

LESSON 15: PRESENT CONTINUOUS TENSE IN KOREAN

In this lesson, we will learn about the helping verbs indicating the present continuous tense in Korean. The present continuous tense is the "-ing" form in English, such as "running" and "jumping." There are two present continuous helping verbs. One is "-고 있다" and another is "-어 /-아 있다." Let us see how we can use them in sentences.

-고 있다

The helping verb "-고 있다" indicates the *present continuous tense* in Korean. It is used after an infinitive of a verb. Let us look at how to use "-고 있다" in sentences.

How to use the helping verb "-고 있다"

1) To indicate a behavior happening now

Listen to Track 146

The helping verb "-고 있다" can mean **be + present particle** in English. It indicates ongoing behaviors in sentences.

- 그는 음악을 **듣고 있다**. *(He is listening to music.)*

    "-고 있다" is used after the infinitive "듣-" of the verb "듣다 (listen)." The basic form of the verb "듣다" is transformed into the present continuous form "듣고 있다."

- 내 동생은 피자를 **먹고있다**. *(My brother is eating a pizza.)*

    "-고 있다" is used after the infinitive "먹-" of the verb "먹다 (eat)." The basic form of the verb "먹다" is transformed into the present continuous form "먹고 있다."

- 친구는 버스를 **기다리고 있다**. *(My friend **is waiting** for a bus.)*

"-고 있다" is used after the infinitive "기다리-" of the verb "기다리다 (wait)." The basic form of the verb "기다리다" is transformed into the present continuous form "기다리고 있다."

2)To indicate a behavior happening now (in videos or pictures)

Listen to Track 147

"-고 있다" can also indicate an ongoing behavior in the news, TV shows, or pictures, even though it happened in the past.

- (Showing her in a TV show) 그녀는 평소처럼 한국어 수업에 **가고 있다**. *(She **is going** to the Korean class as usual.)*

   Even though she already went to the Korean class, it is an ongoing action in the TV show. Thus, you can use "-고 있다."

- (Showing a police officer in the news) 한 경찰관이 강도를 **체포하고 있다**. *(A police officer **is arresting** the robber.)*

   Even though he arrested the robber in the past, it is an ongoing action in the news. Thus, you can use "-고 있다."

- (Pointing a woman in the drawing) 한 여자가 꽃을 **들고 있다**. *(A woman **is holding** a flower.)*

   You can also describe the behavior of a character in a picture.

3) To indicate the short-term

Listen to Track 148

The helping verb "-고 있다" can also describe things happening in the short-term. You can use the present tense for a behavior that hasn't been going on for very long, or something on a temporary basis.

- 나는 요즘 한국어를 공부하**고 있다**. **(Natural)** *(I **am studying** Korean these days .)*
- 나는 지금 밥을 먹**고 있어요**. **(Natural)** *(I'm eating right now.)*
- 나는 최근 삼 개월 동안 중국어를 공부하**고 있다**. **(Natural)** *(I have been learning Chinese for the last three months.)*
- 나는 최근 삼 개월 동안 한국어를 공부**한다**. **(Unnatural)** *(I study Korean for the last three months.)*

In most cases, you will be able to use the present tense and the present continuous tense interchangeably. When a specific range of time is presented, however, it sounds unnatural to use the present tense.

-어 / -아 있다

While the helping verb -고 있다 indicates ongoing behaviors, -어 / -아 있다 indicates an ongoing status. It is used after an infinitive of a verb. Let us look at how to use it in sentences.

How to use -어 / -아 있다

	-어 있다	-아 있다
After	An infinitive of a verb that ends **with a vowel**	An infinitive of a verb that ends **with a consonant**
Meaning	An ongoing status	

1) To indicate an ongoing status

Listen to Track 149

It can be tricky to distinguish the helping verbs -고 있다 and -어 / -아 있다 as both of them mean the present continuous tense in Korean. The difference is that -고 있다 is for ongoing behaviors while the helping verb "-어 / 아 있다" is for an ongoing status.

- 나는 밤새도록 깨**어 있었다**. (Correct) (*I was awake [and stayed up] all night.*)

The helping verb -어 있다 is used as the verb "깨다 (be awake)" ends with a vowel. The basic form of the verb "깨다" becomes the present continuous form "깨어 있다."

- 나는 밤새도록 깨**고 있었다**. (Incorrect) (*I was awaking all night.*)

You do not "awake" repeatedly. You awake once and stay awake. Thus, you have to use -어 있다 for the verb "깨다."

Listen to Track 150

- 정원에 꽃이 피**어 있다**. (Correct) (*Flowers **bloomed (and stayed that way)** in the garden.*)

The helping verb -어 있다 is used as the verb "피다 (bloom)" ends without a final consonant. The basic form of the verb "피다" becomes the present continuous form "피어 있다."

- 정원에 꽃이 피**고 있다.** **(Incorrect)** *(Flowers are blooming in the garden.)*

Flowers do not "bloom" repeatedly. They bloom once and stay that way. Thus, you have to use -어 있다 for the verb "피다."

- (Seeing some flowers in the spring) 꽃이 피**고 있다.** **(Correct)** *(The flowers are blooming in the garden [one by one, gradually].)*

In this case, however, you are mentioning the ongoing behavior of "bloom." Thus, you can use -고 있다 in this sentence.

Listen to Track 151

- 고양이가 의자에 앉**아 있다.** **(Correct)** *(The cat sat [and stays that way] on the chair.)*

The helping verb -아 있다 is used as the verb "앉다 (sit)" ends with a final consonant. The basic form of the verb "앉다" becomes the present continuous form "앉아 있다."

- 고양이가 의자에 앉**고 있다.** **(Incorrect)** *(The cat is sitting on the chair.)*

The cat is not sitting repeatedly. It sits once and stays on the chair. Thus, you have to use -아 있다 in this sentence.

- (Pointing the exact moment when the cat is sitting) 고양이가 의자에 앉**고 있다.** **(Correct)** *(The cat is sitting on the chair [at this exact moment].)*

When you indicate the exact moment when the cat is sitting on the chair, you can use -고 있다.

| **Remember:** | *Korean verbs and adjectives do not exactly correspond with English verbs and adjectives. Some intransitive verbs in Korean are transitive verbs in English, for example, and some English verbs are adjectives in Korean. Thus, please check the dictionary for the part of speech of a word and examples of its use.* |

TIME TO PRACTICE!

Present Continuous Tense in Korean

Exercise 1. Make the following sentences into their present continuous form.

1. 그녀는 노래를 부른다. -> 그녀는 노래를 부르 _____.
   (She sings a song. -> She is singing a song.)

2. 나는 버스를 기다린다. -> 나는 버스를 기다리 _____.
   (I wait for a bus. -> I am waiting for a bus.)

3. 내 고양이는 참치를 먹는다. -> 내 고양이는 참치를 먹 _____.
   (My cat eats tuna. -> My cat is eating tuna.)

4. 나는 음악을 듣는다. -> 나는 음악을 듣 _____.
   (I listen to music. -> I am listening to music.)

5. 나는 집에 간다. -> 나는 집에 가 _____.
   (I go home. -> I am going home.)

6. 나는 점심을 먹는다. -> 나는 점심을 먹 _____.
   (I eat lunch. -> I am eating lunch.)

7. 나는 일한다. -> 나는 일하 _____.
   (I work. -> I am working.)

8. 정원에 장미가 핀다. -> 정원에 장미가 피 _____.
   (The roses have bloomed in the garden.)

9. 강아지가 바닥에 앉는다. -> 강아지가 바닥에 앉 _____.
   (A puppy sits on the floor. -> A puppy is sitting on the floor.)

10. 누나는 우유를 마신다. -> 누나는 우유를 마시 _____.
    (My sister drinks milk. -> My sister is drinking milk.)

Exercise 2. Fill in the blanks with the correct present continuous helping verbs to complete the following sentences:

1. 나는 점심을 _____ 고 있었다. *(I was eating lunch.)*
2. 나는 전자음악을 _____ 고 있었다. *(I was listening to electronic music.)*
3. 새가 창문에 앉 _____. *(A bird is sitting on the window.)*
4. 나는 출장을 가 _____. *(I am going on a business trip.)*

5. 나는 하루종일 _____ 고 있었다. *(I was working all day.)*
6. 나는 한국어를 공부하 _____. *(I am studying Korean.)*
7. 나는 학교에 _____ 고 있다. *(I am going to school.)*
8. 내 아버지는 파스타를 요리하 _____. *(My father is cooking pasta.)*
9. 마당에 해바라기가 피 _____. *(Sunflowers have bloomed in the yard.)*
10. 어머니는 책을 읽 _____. *(My mother is reading a book.)*

Exercise 3. Choose the right word in the following sentences:

1. 사자가 바위 위에서 자 **[고 있다 / 어 있다]**. *(A lion is sleeping on the rock.)* _____

2. 집 앞에 예쁜 꽃이 많이 피 **[고 있다 / 어 있다]**. *(Many beautiful flowers have bloomed in front of my house.)* _____

3. 나는 일본에 가 **[고 있다 / 어 있다]**. *(I am going to Japan.)* _____
4. 내 형은 웃 **[고 있다 / 어 있다]**. *(My brother is laughing.)* _____
5. 나는 라면을 요리하 **[고 있다 / 어 있다]**. *(I am cooking ramen.)* _____
6. 기사가 용과 싸우 **[고 있다 / 어 있다]**. *(A knight is fighting a dragon.)* _____

7. 땅이 아직도 젖 **[고 있다 / 어 있다]**. *(The ground is still wet.)* _____
8. 그 책에는 가격표가 붙 **[고 있다 / 어 있다]**. *(There is a price tag on the book.)* _____

9. 나무가 불타 **[고 있다 / 어 있다]**. *(A tree is burning.)* _____
10. 자동차가 빠르게 달리 **[고 있다 / 어 있다]**. *(A car is running fast.)* _____

Exercise 4. Determine if the following sentences are Correct / Incorrect.

1. 나는 밤새도록 깨고 있었다. *(I was awake all night.)* _____
2. 나는 학교에 가어 있었다. *(I was going to school.)* _____
3. 나는 운동하고 있다. *(I am working out.)* _____
4. 사슴이 달리어 있다. *(A deer is running.)* _____
5. 내 동생은 울고 있다. *(My brother is crying.)* _____
6. 나는 친구와 저녁을 먹어 있다. *(I am eating dinner with my friend.)* _____

7. 나는 병원에 가고 있다. *(I am going to the clinic.)* _____
8. 경찰차가 한 차량을 뒤쫓고 있다. *(A police car is chasing the car.)* _____
9. 내 친구는 낮잠 자어 있다. *(My friend is taking a nap.)* _____
10. 내 선생님은 커피를 마시고 있다. *(My teacher is drinking a cup of coffee.)* _____

Exercise 5. Determine if the following statements are True / False:

1. 고 있다 is used after an infinitive of a verb. _____
2. 어 있다 and 아 있다 are different in meaning. _____
3. 고 있다 indicates the ongoing "status." _____
4. 어 있다 can be used after an infinitive that ends without a bottom. _____
5. Both 고 있다 and 어 있다 are helping verbs. _____
6. The present continuous form is identical to the present form in Korean. _____
7. 고 있다 can indicate something that happens on a regular basis. _____
8. 고 있다 cannot indicate an ongoing "behavior." _____
9. A helping verb cannot be used alone without an infinitive. _____
10. 고 있다 can be used after an adjective. _____

ANSWERS:

Exercise 1

1. -고 있다 / 2. -고 있다 / 3. -고 있다 / 4. -고 있다 / 5. -고 있다 / 6. -고 있다 / 7. -고 있다 / 8. -어 있다 / 9. -아 있다 / 10. -고 있다

Exercise 2

1. 먹- / 2. 듣- / 3. -아 있다 / 4. -고 있다 / 5. 일하- / 6. -고 있다 / 7. 가- / 8. -고 있다 / 9. -어 있다 / 10. -고 있다

Exercise 3

1. -고 있다 / 2. -어 있다 / 3. -고 있다 / 4. -고 있다 / 5. -고 있다 / 6. -고 있다 / 7. -어 있다 / 8. -어 있다 / 9. -고 있다 / 10. -고 있다

Exercise 4

1. Incorrect (깨고 -> 깨어) / 2. Incorrect (가어 -> 가고) / 3. Correct / 4. Incorrect (달리어 -> 달리고) / 5. Correct / 6. Incorrect (먹어 -> 먹고) / 7. Correct / 8. Correct / 9. Incorrect (자어 -> 자고) / 10. Correct

Exercise 5

1. True / 2. False (They are the same in meaning.) / 3. False (It indicates ongoing behaviors.) / 4. True / 5. True / 6. False (The present continuous form is not identical to the present form in Korean.) / 7. True / 8. False (It indicates ongoing behaviors.) / 9. True / 10. False (It cannot be used after an adjective.)

QUICK RECAP

Today we learned about the two present continuous helping verbs in Korean. The helping verb -고 있다 indicates an ongoing behavior and the helping verb -어 있다 indicates an ongoing status. You did a good job today!

	-고 있다	-어 있다	-아 있다
After	An infinitive of a verb	An infinitive of a verb that ends without a bottom	An infinitive of a verb that ends with a bottom
Meaning	Ongoing behaviors; habits	Ongoing status	

LESSON 16: RULES TO TURN VERBS INTO NOUNS/GERUNDS

In this lesson, we will learn about how to make gerunds and noun clauses in Korean. While English uses the "-**ing**" form to transform verbs into nouns, Korean uses **postpositions** to make gerunds and noun clauses. Let's see how we can transform verbs into nouns in Korean. This might all sound a little bit tricky, so let's define these complicated terms:

- **Gerund** - a verb that's acting as a noun (I like *running*).
- **Postposition** - a word added after a noun, pronoun, or verb.
- **Noun clause** - a clause that plays the role of a noun (Ex. "Please tell me *who did this*.")

The Postpositions -ㄴ(은) 것 and -는 것

Korean modifies an infinitive of a verb to make a gerund in the same way as English does. While English uses the "-**ing**" to make a gerund, Korean uses the postpositions -ㄴ(은) 것 and -는 것 to make a gerund.

-ㄴ(은) 것 and -는 것 can be used to make noun clauses as well. They work like the relative pronoun "what" in English.

English Gerund	Infinitive of verb + "-ing"
Korean Gerund	**Infinitive of verb + -ㄴ(은) 것 / -는 것**
English Noun Clause	**What + S + V**
Korean Noun Clause	**S + Infinitive of verb + -ㄴ(은) 것 / -는 것**

Like English gerunds and noun clauses, Korean gerunds and noun clauses can be used as subjects, objects, or complements. Let's see how we can make gerunds and noun clauses in Korean and how we can use them in sentences.

How to use -ㄴ(은) 것 and -는 것

To make a verb into a gerund or a noun clause, you have to find the infinitive of the verb first (this is also called the verb **stem**), and then you can add the postpositions. Please note that the postposition -은 것 is used instead of the postposition -ㄴ 것 when a verb stem has a final consonant.

Listen to Track 152

The Postposition -ㄴ (은) 것

- 내가 **먹은 것**은 피자이다. (***What I ate*** *was pizza.*)
  You can add the postposition -ㄴ (은) 것 after the verb stem 먹- of 먹다.
  As the verb stem ends with a consonant, -은 것 is used.

- 내가 **잃어버린 것**은 내 잘못이다. (***What I lost*** *is a key.*)
  You can add -ㄴ (은) 것 after the verb stem 잃어버리- of 잃어버리다.

- 제 지갑을 **훔친 것**을 알아요. (*I know that [you]* ***stole my wallet***.)
  You can add -ㄴ (은) 것 after the verb stem 훔치- of 훔치다. This example uses -ㄴ(은)것 as the object of the sentence and the act of stealing the wallet becomes the noun.

Listen to Track 153

The Postposition -는 것

- 학교에 **지각하는 것**은 나쁜 습관이다. (***Being late*** *for school is a bad habit.*)
  You can add -는 것 after the verb stem 지각하- of 지각하다.

- 일찍 **자는 것**은 건강에 좋다. (***Sleeping*** *early is good for your health.*)
  You can add -는 것 after the verb stem 자- of 자다.

- 그녀는 쇼핑하러 **가는 것**을 좋아한다. (*She likes* ***going shopping***.)
  You can -는 것 after the verb stem 가- of the verb 가다.

The Difference Between -ㄴ (은) 것 and -는 것

Although -ㄴ 것 and -는 것 can be used interchangeably in some sentences, there is a major difference between them: The postposition -는 것 cannot be used when the sentence implies past tense. The postposition -ㄴ(은) 것 implies a past tense while the postposition -는 것 does not.

Listen to Track 154

-ㄴ(은) 것 implies past tense

- 나는 한국어 **공부하는 것**을 좋아한다. **(Correct)** (*I like **studying Korean**.*)
  나는 한국어 **공부한 것**을 좋아한다. **(Incorrect)**

You are talking about your preference in general. Thus, you cannot use the postposition -ㄴ(은) 것 as it implies past tense.

- 나는 늦게 **잔 것**을 후회한다. **(Correct)** (*I regret **sleeping late**.*)
  나는 늦게 **자는 것**을 후회한다. **(Incorrect)**

Listen to Track 155

When you regret something you did in the past, you have to use the postposition -ㄴ(은) 것.

- 학교에 **지각하는 것**은 나쁜 습관이다. **(Correct)** (***Being late for school** is a bad habit.*)
  학교에 **지각한 것**은 나쁜 습관이다. **(Incorrect)**

You are talking about repeated behavior. Thus, you cannot use the postposition -ㄴ 것.

- 열쇠를 **잃어버린 것**은 실수였다. **(Correct)** (***Losing the key** was a mistake.*)
  열쇠를 **잃어버리는 것**은 실수였다. **(Incorrect)**

You lost a key in the past. Thus, you have to use the postposition -ㄴ 것.

The semantic nuances between the two postpositions

Listen to Track 156

- 내가 **좋아한 것**은 딸기이다. (*What I liked was strawberries.*) (Past)
- 내가 **좋아하는 것**은 딸기이다. (*I like strawberries.*) (Present)
- 내가 **먹은 것**은 햄버거이다. (*What I ate was a hamburger.*) (Past)
  내가 **먹는 것**은 햄버거이다. (*What I'm eating is a hamburger.*) (Present)

- 내가 **싫어한 것**은 브로콜리이다. *(What I hated was broccoli.)* (Past)
- 내가 **싫어하는 것**은 브로콜리이다. *(What I hate is broccoli.)* (Present)
- 내가 **산 것**은 김치이다. *(What I bought was Kimchi.)* (Past)
  내가 **사는 것**은 김치이다. *(What I'm buying is Kimchi.)* (Present)

The Postposition -기

English Gerund	Infinitive of verb + "-ing"
Korean Gerund	Infinitive of verb + -기

Another postposition to make gerunds is the postposition -기. You can transform a verb into a noun by adding the postposition -기 after an infinitive of a verb. Let's see how we can use it and how it differs from the other two postpositions.

Listen to Track 157

How to use the postposition "-기"

Examples:

- 한국어를 **공부하기**는 재미있다. ***(Studying Korean** is fun.)*
  You can add -기 after the verb stem 공부하- of 공부하다.
  Here the gerund is used as the subject.

- 그녀는 쇼핑하러 **가기**를 좋아한다. *(She likes **going shopping**.)*
  You can add -기 after the verb stem 가- of 가다.
  Here the gerund is used as an object.

- 내 취미는 피아노 **치기**이다. *(My hobby is **playing the piano**.)*
  You can add -기 after the verb stem 치- of 치다.
  Here the gerund is used as a subject complement.

The difference between -기, -ㄴ (은) 것, and -는 것

While all the three postpositions transform a verb to a noun in Korean, there are major differences between the three postpositions.

-기 cannot be a subject when the subject complement is tangible.

Listen to Track 158

- 내가 **먹은 것**은 피자이다. **(Correct)** *(What I had was pizza.)*
  내가 **먹기**는 피자이다. **(Incorrect)**
  Since the subject complement "pizza" is tangible, you cannot use -기.

- 내가 **좋아하는 것**은 딸기이다. **(Correct)** *(What I like is strawberry.)*
  내가 **좋아하기**는 딸기이다. **(Incorrect)**
  As the subject complement "strawberry" is tangible, you cannot use -기.

- 내가 **싫어하는 것**은 브로콜리이다. **(Correct)** *(What I dislike is broccoli.)*
  내가 **싫어하기**는 브로콜리이다. **(Incorrect)**
  Since the subject complement "broccoli" is tangible, you cannot use -기.

-기 cannot be used when the sentence implies past tense.

Listen To Track 159

- 나는 늦게 **잔 것**을 후회한다. **(Correct)** *(I regret **sleeping late**.)*
  나는 늦게 **자기**를 후회한다. **(Incorrect)**
  You regret that you slept late. Thus, you can use only -ㄴ (은) 것.

Listen To Track 160

- 내가 **본 것**은 작은 고양이였다. **(Correct)** *(What I saw was a little cat.)*
  내가 **보기**는 작은 고양이이다. **(Incorrect)**
  You saw the cat in the past. Thus, you can use only -ㄴ (은) 것.

- 나는 학교에 **지각한 것**을 후회한다. **(Correct)** *(I regret **being late for school**.)*
  나는 학교에 **지각하기**를 후회한다. **(Incorrect)**
  You regret that you were late for school. Thus, you can use only -ㄴ (은) 것.

-기 is used with objects or complements in most sentences.

Even if a subject complement is not tangible, using the postposition -기 for subjects can sound weird in many cases. Thus, it is safer to use the postpositions -ㄴ (은) 것 or -는 것 for subjects.

TIME TO PRACTICE!

Rules to Turn Verbs into Nouns/Gerunds

Exercise 1. Find the verb stem in the following sentences:

1. 나는 피자를 먹는다. -> 내가 먹은 것은 피자이다. _____
   (I eat pizza. -> What I ate was pizza.)

2. 나는 열쇠를 잃어버렸다. -> 내가 잃어버린 것은 열쇠이다. _____
   (I lost a key. -> What I lost is a key.)

3. 나는 작은 고양이를 봤다. -> 내가 본 것은 작은 고양이이다. _____
   (I saw a little cat. -> What I saw was a little cat.)

4. 그녀는 쇼핑하러 가기를 좋아한다. -> 그녀는 쇼핑하러 가는 것을 좋아한다.
   _____
   (She loves going shopping.)

5. 나는 딸기를 좋아한다. -> 내가 좋아하는 것은 딸기이다. _____
   (I like strawberries. -> What I like are strawberries.)

6. 나는 샐러드를 먹었다. -> 내가 먹은 것은 샐러드이다. _____
   (I ate a salad. -> What I ate was a salad.)

7. 나는 새우를 싫어한다. -> 내가 싫어하는 것은 새우이다. _____
   (I do not like shrimp. -> What I dislike is shrimp.)

8. 나는 소세지를 샀다. -> 내가 산 것은 소시지다. _____
   (I bought a sausage. -> What I bought is a sausage.)

9. 나는 피아노 치기를 좋아한다. -> 내가 좋아하는 것은 피아노 치는 것이에요.
   _____
   (I like playing the piano. -> What I like is playing the piano.)

10. 한국어를 공부하는 것은 재미있다. -> 한국어를 공부하기는 재미있다.
    _____
    (What is fun is studying Korean. -> Studying Korean is fun.)

Exercise 2. Choose the right one in the following sentences:

1. 내가 먹 [ㄴ(은) 것 / 기] 은 삼겹살이다. *(What I ate was Korean BBQ.)*
   _____

2. 내가 보 [ㄴ(은) 것 / 기] 은 작은 강아지이다. *(What I saw was a little puppy.)*
   _____

3. 나는 기타 치 [ㄴ(은) 것 / 기] 를 좋아한다. *(I like playing the guitar.)*
   _____

4. 나는 낮잠자 [ㄴ(은) 것 / 기] 를 좋아한다. *(I like taking a nap.)*
   _____

5. 내가 어제 하 [ㄴ(은) 것 / 기] 은 비밀이다. *(What I did yesterday is a secret.)*
   _____

6. 재활용 하 [ㄴ(은) 것 / 기] 는 환경에 좋다. *(Recycling is good for the environment.)* _____

7. 물을 자주 마시 [ㄴ(은) 것 / 기] 는 건강에 좋다. *(Drinking water often is good for health.)* _____

8. 영어를 공부하 [ㄴ(은) 것 / 기] 는 어렵다. *(Studying English is difficult.)*
   _____

9. 내가 사 [ㄴ(은) 것 / 기] 은 컴퓨터이다. *(What I bought is a computer.)*
   _____

10. 컴퓨터를 조립하 [ㄴ(은) 것 / 기] 는 쉽다. *(Assembling a computer is easy.)*
    _____

Exercise 3. Choose the right one in the following sentences:

1. 일찍 자 [ㄴ(은) 것 / 는 것] 은 건강에 좋다. *(Sleeping early is good for health.)*
   _____

2. 나는 늦게 자 [ㄴ(은) 것 / 는 것] 을 후회한다. *(I regret sleeping late last night.)*
   _____

3. 내가 싫어하 [ㄴ(은) 것 / 는 것] 은 거짓말이다. *(What I hate is a lie.)*
   _____

4. 나는 거짓말하 [ㄴ(은) 것 / 는 것] 을 싫어한다. *(I hate lying.)*
   _____

5. 친구와 게임하 [ㄴ(은) 것 / 는 것] 은 재미있다. *(Playing video games with friends is fun.)* _____

6. 나는 거짓말 하 **[ㄴ(은) 것 / 는 것]** 을 후회한다. *(I regret lying.)*

   _____

7. 친구는 등산하 **[ㄴ(은) 것 / 는 것]** 을 좋아한다. *(My friend likes climbing.)*

   _____

8. 내가 잃어버리 **[ㄴ(은) 것 / 는 것]** 은 지갑이다. *(What I lost is a wallet.)*

   _____

9. 내가 어렸을 때 좋아하 **[ㄴ(은) 것 / 는 것]** 은 로봇이다. *(Robots are what I liked when I was young.)* _____

10. 매일 운동 하 **[ㄴ(은) 것 / 는 것]** 은 좋은 습관이다. *(Working out every day is a good habit.)* _____

Exercise 4. Determine if the following sentences are Correct / Incorrect:

1. 늦게 잔 것은 나쁜 습관이다. *(Going to bed late at night is a bad habit.)*

   _____

2. 내가 제일 좋아하는 것은 오렌지 주스이다. *(What I like the most is orange juice.)* _____

3. 나는 일찍 일어나지 않은 것을 후회한다. *(I regret not waking up early.)*

   _____

4. 한국인은 노래방에 간 것을 좋아한다. *(Koreans like going Noraebang [karaoke].)* _____

5. 나는 사우나 가는 것을 좋아한다. *(I like going to the Sauna.)*

   _____

6. 내가 제일 좋아한 것은 콜라이다. *(What I like the most is cola.)*

   _____

7. 내 고양이는 낮잠자는 것을 좋아한다. *(My cat likes taking a nap.)*

   _____

8. 나는 어제 늦게 자는 것을 후회한다. *(I regret sleeping late yesterday.)*

   _____

9. 남에게 욕설을 하는 것은 무례하다. *(Insulting others is rude.)*

   _____

10. 내가 가장 좋아한 것은 레이싱 게임이다. *(What I like most are racing games.)*

   _____

Exercise 5. Determine if the following statements are True / False:

1. When the infinitive has a bottom, you have to use 은 것. _____
2. There is no difference in meaning between 은 것 and 는 것. _____
3. 은 것 implies a future tense. _____
4. 는 것 cannot be used when it implies past tense. _____
5. 기 is connected to an infinitive of a verb. _____
6. 기 can be used as an object. _____
7. 는 것 implies past tense. _____
8. 는 것 can be used as a subject. _____
9. An infinitive of a verb is not a present form of a verb. _____
10. 기 cannot be used when it implies past tense. _____

ANSWERS:

Exercise 1

1. 먹- / 2. 잃어버리- / 3. 보- / 4. 가- / 5. 좋아하- / 6. 먹- / 7. 싫어하- / 8. 사- / 9. 치- / 10. 공부하-

Exercise 2

1. ㄴ(은) 것 / 2. ㄴ(은) 것 / 3. 기 / 4. 기 / 5. ㄴ(은) 것 / 6. 기 / 7. 기 / 8.기 / 9. ㄴ(은) 것 / 10. 기

Exercise 3

1. 는 것 / 2. ㄴ(은) 것 / 3. 는 것 / 4. 는 것 / 5. 는 것 / 6. ㄴ(은) 것 / 7. 는 것 / 8. ㄴ(은) 것 / 9. ㄴ(은) 것 / 10. 는 것

Exercise 4

1. Incorrect (잔 것은 -> 자는 것은) / 2. Correct / 3. Correct / 4. Incorrect (간 것을 -> 가는 것을) / 5. Correct / 6. Incorrect (좋아한 것은 -> 좋아하는 것은) / 7. Correct / 8. Incorrect (자는 것을 -> 잔 것을) / 9. Correct / 10. Incorrect (좋아한 것은 -> 좋아하는 것은)

Exercise 5

1. True / 2. False ("은 것" implies past tense while "는 것" does not.) / 3. False ("은 것" implies past tense.) / 4. True / 5. True / 6. True / 7. False ("는 것" does not imply past tense.) / 8. True / 9. True / 10. True

QUICK RECAP

Today you learned how to make gerunds and noun clauses in Korean. It is useful to use gerunds and noun clauses as you can make a noun from a verb without memorizing another word. Please review and practice. You did a good job today!

	ㄴ(은) 것	-는 것	-기
Making	Noun Clause / Gerund		Gerund
Meaning	What S + V / V -ing		V -ing
Part of Sentence	Tangible Subject Object Complement		Intangible Subject Object Complement
Implying	Past Tense	Present / Future Tense	

LESSON 17: INTRODUCTION TO KOREAN CONJUNCTIONS

In this lesson, we will introduce you to Korean conjunctions. There are many different conjunctions in the Korean language, some of which mean the same thing. How and when to use each depends on the situation, and to whom you're speaking.

It may sound confusing at first, but you will have a better understanding by the end of this lesson!

Ways to Say "And"

There are four different ways to say the word "and" in Korean. Three of them are very similar and are used to link words together, and one of them is used to link two separate independent clauses or sentences.

To link two words or phrases together with "and" in Korean:

- 와/과 - use 와 after a vowel and 과 after a consonant
- (이)랑 - use 랑 after a vowel and 이랑 after a consonant
- 하고

The Postpositions 와 / 과

The postpositions 와 / 과 are conjunctive postpositions. They mean the preposition "with" or the conjunction "and" in English. Let us see how you can use them in sentences.

How to Use 와 / 과

	-와	-과
After	A noun or a pronoun that ends **with a vowel**	A noun or a pronoun that ends **with a consonant**
Meaning	And With	

To mean the English preposition "with"

Listen to Track 161

- 그는 **아내와** 산책을 했다. *(He took a walk **with** his wife.)*
  As 아내 is a noun that ends with a vowel, 와 is used.

- 어제 나는 **친구들과** 테니스를 쳤다. *(Yesterday I played tennis **with** my friends.)*
  As 친구들 is a noun that ends with a final consonant, 과 is used.

To mean the English conjunction "and"

Listen to Track 162

- 개와 고양이 -> 개, 고양이 *(A dog **and** a cat -> A dog, a cat)*
  You can put a comma (,) instead of 와 / 과.

- **나와** 레이첼은 좋은 친구이다. -> **레이첼과** 나는 좋은 친구이다. *(I **and** Rachel are good friends. -> Rachel **and** I are good friends.)*
  Even though the meaning of sentences are the same, different postpositions are used as 나 (I) ends with a vowel and 레이첼 (Rachel) ends with a final consonant.

The Postposition (이)랑

The postpositions **이랑** and **랑** are conjunctive postpositions. They work in the same way as the postpositions 와 / 과 do. The slight difference is that 이랑 and 랑 are mainly used in informal and spoken conversations.

Listen to Track 163

How to Use (이)랑

	-랑	**-이랑**
After	A noun or a pronoun that ends **with a vowel**	A noun or a pronoun that ends **with a consonant**
Meaning	And With	

To mean the English preposition "with"

- 그는 **강아지랑** 산책을 했다. *(He took a walk **with** his dog.)*
  As 강아지 is a noun that ends with a vowel, 랑 is used.

- 어제 나는 **친구들이랑** 축구를 했다. *(Yesterday I played soccer **with** my friends.)*
  As 친구들 is a noun that ends with a final consonant, 이랑 is used.

To mean the English conjunction "and"

Listen to Track 164

- 원숭이**랑** 코끼리 -> 원숭이, 코끼리 *(A monkey **and** an elephant -> A monkey, an elephant)*
  You can put a comma (,) instead of (이)랑.

- **나랑** 아일린은 좋은 친구이다. -> **아일린이랑** 나는 좋은 친구이다. *(I **and** Aylin are good friends. -> Alyin **and** I are good friends.)*
  When there is no final consonant, 랑 should be used. When there is a final consonant, 이랑 should be used.

The Postposition 하고

The postposition 하고 works in the same way as 와 / 과 and (이)랑 do. The difference is that 하고 **is only for spoken conversations**. You will not see the postposition 하고 in texts except for poems or novels.

Listen to Track 165

How to Use 하고

The postposition 하고 can be placed after any noun or pronoun.

To mean the English preposition "with"

- 내 누나는 **강아지하고** 산책을 했다. *(My sister took a walk **with** her dog.)*
- 지난 주 나는 **친구들하고** 게임을 했다. *(Last week I played video games **with** my friends.)*

To mean the English conjunction "and"

Listen to Track 166

- 계란**하고** 우유 -> 계란, 우유 *(An egg **and** milk -> An egg, milk)*
  You can put a comma (,) instead of 하고.

- **나하고** 데이빗은 좋은 친구이다. -> **데이빗하고** 나는 좋은 친구이다. *(I **and** David are good friends. -> David **and** I are good friends.)*
  "하고" can be used with or without a final consonant.

Listen to Track 167

Combining Conjunctions with 함께/같이

When the words are used as "with" instead of "and," the word "together" is often included as well and translates as "together with." There are two Korean words for "together" that can be used interchangeably: 같이 and 함께.

- 친구**랑 같이** 점심을 먹었어요. *(I ate lunch **together with** a friend.)*
- 김치는 밥**하고 같이** 드세요. *(Please eat kimchi **together with** rice.)*
- 식구들**과 함께** 여행을 갔었어요. *(I traveled **together with** my family.)*

When you see the words 같이 or 함께 along with 하고/(이)랑/과/와, it should always be translated as "together with."

Listen to Track 168

Korean Conjunction "and" – 그리고

The word "그리고" is used between sentences to link two independent clauses together in Korean. The word signifies that a new thought or a sentence is about to begin.

Below are some examples:

- 짜장면 두 그릇 주세요. **그리고** 군만두도 주세요. *(Please give us two orders of Jjajangmyun. **And** give us pan-fried dumplings.)*
- 오늘은 금요일이에요. **그리고** 내일은 쉬는 날이에요. *(Today is Friday. **And** tomorrow is a rest day.)*

- 그 골목길은 사람들이 많이 안 다녀요. **그리고** 너무 어두워요. (*Not too many people use that alleyway.* **And** *it is too dark.*)

The use of 그리고 is very straightforward. You just take two sentences that you want to link, and add the word 그리고 at the beginning of the second sentence. There is, however, a way to simplify the two sentences and make them into one. But that requires more advanced grammar and we will skip it for now.

Now let's look at some additional Korean conjunctions.

Listen to Track 169

Korean Conjunction "so" – 그래서

The Korean conjunction 그래서 meaning "so" or "therefore," is placed between sentences and links independent clauses together, much like the Korean words for "and." Korean doesn't make use of commas often, so conjunctions can take on the function of what we would attribute to a comma. Which is why in the examples below, the English translation contains a comma but the Korean does not. When using conjunctions in Korean, you'll most often find them at the start of a separate sentence.

Here are some examples:

- 저는 돈이 없어요. **그래서** 쇼핑을 못가요. (*I don't have money,* **so** *I can't go shopping.*)
- 어제는 너무 많이 먹었어요. **그래서** 오늘 배가 아파요. (*I ate too much yesterday,* **so** *my stomach hurts today.*)
- 공부를 안 했어요. **그래서** 시험 성적이 안 좋아요. (*I did not study,* **so** *my test score was not good.*)

Listen to Track 170

Korean Conjunction "but" - 그러나 / 하지만 / 그렇지만 / 그런데

There are four different words to indicate "but" or "however" in Korean:

- 그러나
- 하지만
- 그렇지만
- 그런데

All four of them can be used interchangeably when two sentences have contrasting information, as shown below:

Listen to Track 171

- 레몬은 셔요. **그러나** 오렌지는 달아요. _(Lemons are sour, **but** oranges are sweet.)_
- 저는 오늘 아파요. **그렇지만** 일하러 가야 해요. _(I am sick today, **but** I have to go to work.)_
- 날씨가 추워요. **하지만** 밖에서 테니스를 칠 거예요. _(The weather is cold, **but** we will play tennis outside.)_
- 배가 고파요. **그런데** 점심 먹을 시간이 없어요. _(I am hungry. **But** there is no time to eat lunch.)_

However, the second sentence does not necessarily contain contrasting information after the word "but." Instead, it can contain additional information about or in relation to the previous sentence.

The "but" can also be understood as "and by the way." In such instances, #4 (**그런데**) is used.

For example:

Listen to Track 172

- 어제 과일을 샀어요. **그런데** 싱싱하지 않아요.
  (I bought some fruit yesterday, **but** it is not very fresh.)
  (I bought some fruit yesterday, and by the way, it is not very fresh.)

- 오늘 영화를 봤어요. **그런데** 재미없었어요.
  (I watched a movie today, **but** it was not very good.)
  (I watched a movie today, and by the way, it was not very good.)

- 밤새도록 공부했어요. **그런데** 늦잠을 자서 시험을 못 봤어요.
  (I studied all night, **but** I overslept and missed the test.)
  (I studied all night, and unfortunately, I overslept and missed the test.)

그런데 is probably the most often used conjunction for "but" in conversation. However, you should remember that 그런데 can have two different meanings depending on the context.

The good news is that since 그런데 can be used for both "but" and "by the way," you can just default to 그런데 when composing your own sentences until you become more advanced in the Korean language.

TIME TO PRACTICE!

Introduction to Korean Conjunctions

Exercise 1. Choose 와 or 과 in the following sentences:

1. 개는 늑대 **[와 / 과]** 비슷하게 생겼다. *(A dog resembles a wolf.)* _____
2. 친구들 **[와 / 과]** 공부를 했다. *(I studied with my friends.)* _____
3. 나는 친구 **[와 / 과]** 산책을 했다. *(I took a walk with my friend.)* _____
4. 나는 누나 **[와 / 과]** 청소를 했다. *(I cleaned the house with my sister.)* _____
5. 기린 **[와 / 과]** 사자가 있다. *(There is a giraffe and a lion.)* _____
6. 레이첼 **[와 / 과]** 나는 고등학교 친구이다. *(Rachel and I are high school friends.)* _____
7. 점심에 튀김 **[와 / 과]** 햄버거를 먹었다. *(I ate fries and a hamburger for lunch.)* _____
8. 사자 **[와 / 과]** 기린이 있다. *(There is a lion and a giraffe.)* _____
9. 자유 **[와 / 과]** 평등은 중요한 가치이다. *(Liberty and equality are important values.)* _____
10. 나는 직장 동료 **[와 / 과]** 결혼했다. *(I married my coworker.)* _____

Exercise 2. Choose 랑 or 이랑 in the following sentences:

1. 나는 동생 **[랑 / 이랑]** 수영장에 다녀왔다. *(I went to a swimming pool with my brother.)* _____
2. 나는 아버지 **[랑 / 이랑]** 닮았다. *(I resemble my father.)* _____
3. 나는 친구들 **[랑 / 이랑]** 영화관에 갔다. *(I went to the cinema with my friends.)* _____
4. 오드리 **[랑 / 이랑]** 나는 대학교 친구이다. *(Audrey and I are college friends.)* _____
5. 개 **[랑 / 이랑]** 고양이는 보통 사이가 좋지 않다. *(A dog and a cat usually do not get along well.)* _____
6. 기린 **[랑 /이랑]** 사자는 아프리카에 산다. *(Giraffes and lions live in Africa.)* _____
7. 나 **[랑 / 이랑]** 같이 도서관에 갈래? *(Do you want to go to the library with me?)* _____

8. 동생 **[랑 / 이랑]** 나는 사이가 좋다. *(I get along with my sister well.)* _____

9. 아버지 **[랑 / 이랑]** 어머니는 대학교에서 처음 만났다. *(My father and mother met each other at college.)* _____

10. 내 동생은 인형 **[랑 / 이랑]** 놀고 있다. *(My sister is playing with dolls.)* _____

Exercise 3. Determine if the following statements are True / False:

1. Using 하고 is recommended for formal and written conversation. _____
2. 와 and 과 can be used only for spoken conversation. _____
3. 랑 and 이랑 cannot be used for spoken conversation. _____
4. 며 and 이며 have the meaning of the word "with." _____
5. 에 does not have the meaning of the word "with." _____
6. 며 and 이며 cannot connect objects. _____
7. 며 and 이며 can connect subjects. _____
8. 하고 means both "and" and "with." _____
9. When a noun ends with a vowel, you cannot use 에. _____
10. 하고 can be used regardless of the final consonant of a noun. _____

Exercise 4. Fill in the blanks in the following sentences:

1. 나는 남편 _____ 산책을 했다. *(I took a walk with my husband.)*
2. 나는 내일 친구들 _____ 골프를 칠 것이다.
   (Tomorrow I am going to play golf with my friends.)
3. 내 동생은 강아지 _____ 공원에서 놀았다.
   (My brother and his dog played in the park.)
4. 나 _____ 엘리자베스는 좋은 친구이다. *(I and Elizabeth are good friends.)*
5. 나는 아버지 _____ 어머니를 사랑한다. *(I love my father and mother.)*
6. 은화 _____ 금괴 _____ 보물로 가득찬 방.
   (The room was filled with treasures such as silver coins and gold bars.)
7. 동생은 치킨 _____ 피자 _____ 맛있는 음식을 많이 먹었다.
   (My brother ate many delicious foods including pizza and fried chicken.)
8. 어머니는 계란 _____ 우유를 샀다. *(My mother bought eggs and milk.)*
9. 데이빗은 나 _____ 같은 회사에서 일한다.
   (David and I are working in the same company.)
10. 형 _____ 나는 닮았다. *(I resemble my brother.)*

Exercise 5. Determine if the following sentences are Correct / Incorrect:

1. 나는 어머니며 아버지며 사랑한다. *(I love my mother and father.)*_____
2. 나는 아버지에 어머니에 사랑한다. *(I love my father and mother.)*_____
3. 나는 어머니와 아버지를 사랑한다. *(I love my father and mother.)*_____
4. 나에 신디에 좋은 친구이다. *(I and Cindy are good friends.)* _____
5. 내 누나는 고양이와 강아지를 기른다. *(My sister has a cat and a dog.)* _____
6. 계란와 우유 *(An egg and milk)*_____
7. 나는 친구들랑 게임을 했다. *(I played video games with my friends.)* _____
8. 마우스이랑 키보드 *(A mouse and a keyboard)*_____
9. 나는 수학과 과학을 좋아한다. *(I like mathematics and science.)*_____
10. 개이랑 고양이 *(A dog and a cat)*_____

Exercise 6. Find the conjunctions in the following sentences:

1. 저는 친구랑 점심을 먹었어요. -> _____ *(I had lunch with my friend.)*
2. 김치는 밥하고 드세요. -> _____ *(Please eat Kimchi with rice.)*
3. 저는 가족과 여행을 갔어요. -> _____ *(I traveled with my family.)*
4. 저는 교수님과 저녁을 먹었어요. -> _____ *(I had dinner with my professor.)*
5. 커피 두 잔 주세요. 그리고 케이크도 하나 주세요. -> _____
6. *(Two coffees please. And one cake too.)*
7. 오늘은 일요일이에요. 그리고 내일은 월요일이에요. -> _____
8. *(Today is Sunday. And tomorrow is Monday.)*
9. 겨울 밤은 너무 춥고 어두워요. -> _____ *(Winter nights are so cold and dark.)*
10. 저는 오렌지를 좋아해요. 하지만 딸기는 좋아하지 않아요. -> _____
11. *(I like oranges. But I do not like strawberries.)*
12. 저는 졸려요. 그렇지만 학교에 가야해요. -> _____ *(I am sleepy. But I must go to school.)*
13. 어제 영화를 봤어요. 그런데 너무 지루했어요. -> _____ *(I watched a movie yesterday. But It was so boring.)*

ANSWERS:

Exercise 1

1. 와 / 2. 과 / 3. 와 / 4. 와 / 5. 과 / 6. 과 / 7. 과 / 8. 와 / 9. 와 / 10. 와

Exercise 2

1. 이랑 / 2. 랑 / 3. 이랑 / 4. 랑 / 5. 랑 / 6. 이랑 / 7. 랑 / 8. 이랑 / 9. 랑 /
10. 이랑

Exercise 3

1. False / 2. False / 3. False / 4. False / 5. True / 6. True / 7. False / 8. True /
9. False / 10. True

Exercise 4

1. 과 (이랑, 하고) / 2. 과 (이랑, 하고) / 3. 와 (랑, 하고) / 4. 와 (랑, 하고) /
5. 와 (랑, 하고) / 6. 며 (에) / 7. 며 (에) / 8. 과 (이랑, 하고) / 9. 와 (랑, 하고) /
10. 과 (이랑, 하고)

Exercise 5

1. Incorrect (어머니며 아버지며 -> 어머니와 아버지를) / 2. Incorrect
(아버지에 어머니에 -> 아버지와 어머니를) / 3. Correct / 4. Incorrect (나에
신디에 -> 나와 신디는) / 5. Correct / 6. Incorrect (계란와 -> 계란과) /
7. Incorrect (친구들랑 -> 친구들이랑) / 8. Incorrect (마우스이랑 -> 마우스랑) /
9. Correct / 10. Incorrect (개이랑 -> 개랑)

Exercise 6

1. 랑 / 2. 하고 / 3. 과 / 4. 과 / 5. 그리고 / 6. 그리고 / 7. 고 / 8. 하지만 /
9. 그렇지만 / 10. 그런데

QUICK RECAP

Today you learned about Korean conjunctions. Please check the summary of this lesson below since it can be confusing to learn so many postpositions in a day. See you in the next lesson. You did a great job today!

Listen to Track 173

	Placement	**Meaning**
-와 -랑	After a noun or a pronoun that ends without a bottom	and with (랑 for informal speech)
-과 -이랑	After a noun or a pronoun that ends with a bottom	and with (이랑 for informal speech)
-하고	After a noun or a pronoun	and with (spoken conversation)
그리고	Start of a new sentence	And
그래서	Start of a new sentence	So
그런데	Start of a new sentence	But

LESSON 18: WHO, WHAT, WHEN, WHERE, WHY, AND HOW

There are six basic words in any language that you need to know in order to ask questions. They are: **Who**, **What**, **When**, **Where**, **Why**, and **How**. This lesson will introduce you to the basic Korean question words with a brief explanation of each.

The six Korean words below, along with some basic vocabulary, will give you the ability to ask just about any common question you might have while conversing with a Korean speaker.

Listen to Track 174

Who	누구
What	뭐
When	언제
Where	어디
Why	왜
How	어떻게

These words can be used with various Korean particles to give them different roles in sentences, such as 은/는, 이/가, 을/를, 에, 에서, and so on.

Let's take a look at some examples of each of the question words.

Listen to Track 175

Who – 누구

Sentence	Pronunciation	English Translation
누구를 찾으세요?	[누구를 차즈세요]	*Who are you looking for?* (You is implied. "를" is the object marker for "누구.")
이 사람은 누구예요?	[이 사라믄 누구예요]	*Who is this person?*
이 분은 누구세요?	[이 부는 누구세요]	*Who is this person?* (This has the exact same meaning as above, but this form is used when referring to someone who should be respected due to age, position, or rank.)
누구세요?		*Who are you?* ("You" is implied. You would ask this when answering the phone if you don't know who is calling, or if a stranger approaches you.)

Listen to Track 176

누가 아까 전화 했었어요?	[누가 아까 저놔 해써써요]	*Who called earlier?* ("누가" is the contraction for "누구가," with "가" as the subject particle.)
누구를 추천하세요?	[누구를 추처나세요]	*Who do you recommend?* ("You" is the implied subject, and "who" is the object of the sentence.)
누구는 선물을 주고 누구는 안주고 하는게 불공평해요.	[누구는 선무를 주고 누구는 안주고 하는게 불공평해요]	*It is not fair that some people receive a gift and some people don't.**

*Notice that in the last sentence, the word 누구 is translated as "some people." We wanted to show you an example of using the word with the particle 는.

When a question is being asked with a question word as the subject, the subject particle "가" will almost always be used. The only time the particle 는 is used is when the sentence is comparing and contrasting.

In the above sentence, "some people who receive a gift" and "some people who don't" are being compared. This sentence is actually not a question but a statement, in that the word 누구 is referring to an ambiguous "who," making "some people" the more accurate translation.

In fact, if you ever see the word "누구" with the particle "는," the likely translation will be "someone" or "some people."

Listen to Track 177

What – 뭐

The most used form of the Korean word for "what" is "뭐." The original form of the word is "무엇," but it is transformed as: 무엇 → 무어 → 뭐. In formal writing, 무엇 is still the proper form.

Sentence	Pronunciation	English translation
이게 **뭐**예요?	[이게 모에요]	**What** is this?
이 식당에 **뭐가** 제일 맛있어요?	[이 식땅에 모가 제일 마시써요]	**What** tastes best at this restaurant? ("가" is the subject marker for "뭐.")
그게 **무엇인지** 알려주세요.*	[그게 무어신지 알려주세요]	*Please let me know* **what that is**.
뭘 좋아하세요?*	[몰 조아하세요]	**What** do you like? ("You" is implied.)

Listen to Track 178

*In the last sentence, 뭘 is the contraction for 무엇을:

무엇을 → 무어를 → 무얼 → 뭘.

*Similarly, in the third sentence, 무엇인지 can be contracted to 뭔지.

무엇인지 → 무어인지 → 무언지 → 뭔지

Listen to Track 179

When – 언제

Sentence	Pronunciation	English translation
우리 언제 만날까요?	[우리 언제 만날까요]	*When should we meet?*
언제 다시 오실거예요?	[언제 다시 오실꺼예요]	*When will you come again?* ("You" is implied.)
언제가 제일 좋은지 알려주세요.*	[언제가 제일 조은지 알려주세요]	*Please let me know when is a good time.* ("가" is the subject particle for "언제.")
저는 한식은 언제든지 먹을 수 있어요.*	[저는 한시근 언제든지 머글쑤 이써요]	*I can eat Korean food any time.*

Listen to Track 180

* Notice that the last two sentences are statements rather than questions.

The third sentence, "언제가 제일 좋은지 알려주세요," has the phrase "when is a good time" as the information that the speaker wants to know.

- 언제가 제일 좋아요? + 알려주세요. = 언제가 제일 좋은지 알려주세요.

Listen to Track 181

In the last sentence, the Korean particle "든지" is used with "언제" (when). The particle "든지" is usually used with a question word to indicate "*every* or *any.*"

- 누구든지 *(anyone)*
- 뭐든지 *(anything)*
- 언제든지 *(any time)*
- 어디든지 *(anywhere, everywhere)*
- 어떻게든지 *(any way or every way possible)*

Listen to Track 182

Where – 어디

Sentence	Pronunciation	English translation
어디 가세요?	[어디 가세요]	*Where are you going?* ("You" is implied.)
어디에 있어요?	[어디에 이써요]	*Where is it?* ("It" is implied.)
어디세요?	[어디세요]	*Where are you?* ("You" is implied.)
어디가 제일 맛있어요?	[어디가 제일 마시써요]	*Where is the best tasting food?* ("가" is the subject particle.)
어디로 여행 가고 싶어요?	[어디로 여행 가고 시퍼요]	*Where do you want to travel to?* ("You" is implied. "로" is the particle meaning "to.")
어디에서 왔어요?	[어디에서 와써요]	*Where did you come from?* ("에서" is the particle meaning "from.")

Listen to Track 183

Why – 왜

Sentence	Pronunciation	English translation
왜 전화 했어요?	[왜 저놔 해써요]	*Why did you call?* ("You" is implied.)
왜 이렇게 늦었어요?	[왜 이러케 느저써요]	*Why are you so late?* ("You" is implied.)
왠지 모르겠어요.*	[왠지 모르게써요]	*I don't know why.* ("I" is implied.)

*In the last sentence, the particle "~ㄴ지" is used with "왜," making it "왠지." The particle is used to combine the two parts of the sentence: Why? + I don't know = I don't know why.

Listen to Track 184

How – 어떻게

Sentence	Pronunciation	English translation
그 요리는 어떻게 만들어요?	[그 요리는 어떠케 만드러써요]	*How is that dish made?*
어떻게 하면 성공할 수 있어요?	[어떠케 하면 성공할 쑤 이써요]	*How can I succeed? ("I" is implied.)*
제가 어떻게 도와 드릴까요?	[제가 어떠케 도와 드릴까요]	*How can I help you? ("You" is implied.)*
어떻게 그 사람을 안 도와줄 수가 있어요?	[어떠케 그 사라믈 안 도와줄 쑤가 이써요]	*How can (you/anyone) not help that person?*
어떻게든지 그 사람을 도와주세요.*	[어떠케든지 그 사라믈 도와주세요]	*Please help that person any way possible.*

* As with the last example sentence under "언제" (when), the particle "든지" is used above with "어떻게" (how), and literally translates as "any/every how," meaning "however possible."

TIME TO PRACTICE!

Who, What, When, Where, Why, and How

Exercise 1. Write down the meaning of the question words:

1. 누구 = _____
2. 뭐 = _____
3. 언제 = _____
4. 어디 = _____
5. 왜 = _____
6. 어떻게 = _____

Exercise 2. Put the correct question word [누구 / 뭐 / 언제] in the blank:

1. _____ 를 찾으세요? *(Who are you looking for?)*
2. _____ 부터 여기에 계셨나요? *(Since when have you been here?)*
3. 이 상자는 _____ 에요? *(What is this box?)*
4. _____ 라고 했어요? *(What did you say?)*
5. _____ 저녁 먹을 거에요? *(When will you have dinner?)*
6. 이번 "최고의 여배우" 후보자에 _____ 를 추천하나요? *(Who do you recommend for the "best actress" award nominees?)*
7. 저 청바지를 입은 여자는 _____ 에요? *(Who is that girl in the jeans?)*
8. _____ 든지 물어보세요. *(Ask whatever you want.)*
9. _____ 까지 일 해야 해요? *(Until when do you have to work?)*
10. _____ 든지 찾아오세요. *(Come whenever you want.)*

Exercise 3. Put the right question word [어디 / 왜 / 어떻게] in the blank:

1. _____ 그런 짓을 했나요? *(Why did you do that?)*
2. _____ 나한테 이럴 수 있어! *(How could you do that to me!)*
3. _____ 브로콜리를 싫어하나요? *(Why do you dislike broccoli?)*
4. 이 응용 프로그램을 _____ 설치하나요? *(How can I install this application?)*
5. _____ 여기 계세요? *(Why are you here?)*
6. _____ 하는 지 모르겠어요. *(I do not know how to do it.)*
7. _____ 계세요? *(Where are you?)*
8. _____ 서 만날까요? *(Where shall we meet?)*
9. _____ 로 가는 중이세요? *(Where are you going?)*
10. _____ 말 하지 않았어요? *(Why did you not say that?)*

Exercise 4. Choose the right question word to complete the sentences:

1. **[누구 / 뭐]** 를 먹고 싶으세요? *(What do you want to eat?)* _____

2. **[누구 / 뭐]** 와 함께 갔나요? *(Who did you go with?)* _____

3. 운동이면 **[누구 / 뭐]** 든지 좋아요. *(I like any sport.)* _____

4. **[누구 / 뭐]** 를 만나고 오셨어요? *(Who did you meet?)* _____

5. 고양이 카페가 **[언제 / 어디]** 에 있나요? *(Where is the Kitty Café?)* _____

6. 영화를 보려면 **[언제 / 어디]** 로 가야 하나요? *(Where should I go to watch a movie?)* _____

7. **[언제 / 어디]** 든지 연락하세요. *(Call me whenever you want.)* _____

8. 그녀가 **[왜 / 어떻게]** 그랬는지는 모르겠어요. *(I do not know why she did that.)* _____

9. **[왜 / 어떻게]** 이 문제를 해결할 수 있을까요? *(How can I solve this problem?)* _____

10. **[왜 / 어떻게]** 하면 한국어를 잘 할 수 있을까요? *(How can I become fluent in Korean?)* _____

Exercise 5. Determine if the following sentences are Correct / Incorrect:

1. 무엇이든지 파는 상인이 있어요. *(There is a merchant selling whatever you want.)* _____

2. 나는 어디로 가야하는지 몰라요. *(I do not know where I should go.)* _____

3. 이 식당에서 누가 제일 맛있어요? *(What is the specialty of this restaurant?)* _____

4. 내 고양이는 볼 때마다 때마다 낮잠을 자고 있다. *(My cat is taking a nap whenever I see her.)* _____

5. 왜 그런 말씀을 이제 하세요? *(Why are you saying that now?)* _____

6. 이 물건은 왜에요? *(What is this thing?)* _____

7. 어디가 가장 싼 모델인가요? *(What is the cheapest model?)* _____

8. 언제에서 그 사건이 발생했나요? *(Where did the incident occur?)* _____

9. 어디가 가장 용감한 기사인가요? *(Who is the bravest knight?)* _____

10. 누가 여왕인가요? *(Who is the queen?)* _____

ANSWERS:

Exercise 1

1. Who / 2. What / 3. When / 4. Where / 5. Why / 6. How

Exercise 2

1. 누구 / 2. 언제 / 3. 뭐 / 4. 뭐 / 5. 언제 / 6. 누구 / 7. 누구 / 8. 뭐 / 9. 언제 / 10. 언제

Exercise 3

1. 왜 / 2. 어떻게 / 3. 왜 / 4. 어떻게 / 5. 왜 / 6. 어떻게 / 7. 어디 / 8. 어디 / 9. 어디 / 10. 왜

Exercise 4

1. 뭐 / 2. 누구 / 3. 뭐 / 4. 누구 / 5. 어디 / 6. 어디 / 7. 언제 / 8. 왜 / 9. 어떻게 / 10. 어떻게

Exercise 5

1. Correct / 2. Correct / 3. Incorrect: 누가 (who) -> 뭐가 (what) / 4. Correct / 5. Correct / 6. Incorrect: 왜 (why) -> 뭐 (what) / 7. Incorrect: 어디 (where) -> 뭐 (what) / 8. Incorrect: 언제 (when) -> 어디 (where) / 9. Incorrect: 어디 (where) -> 누가 (who) / 10. Correct

QUICK RECAP

In this lesson, we talked about the six basic question words: Who, What, When, Where, Why, and How. There are several more Korean question words in addition to the six that we have covered in this lesson, but these are the ones most commonly used that you should know.

Once you memorize the six words, you can easily ask simple questions without even knowing how to make a full sentence.

You could point to a picture of a toilet and ask, "어디?" (Where?), and communicate that you are looking for a bathroom. You could point to a person and ask, "누구?" (Who?), and communicate that you want to know who that person is.

You won't have to worry about being lost somewhere in Seoul and having no idea how to ask a question!

LESSON 19: LOCATION MARKERS -에/-에서

Korean uses location markers after a noun or pronoun to indicate locations. There are two specific postpositions for locations; one is -에 and the other is -에서. In this lesson, we will learn all about it.

What Are -에 and -에서?

-에 and -에서 are location marking particles. They transform a noun or pronoun into an adverb indicating location. These particles work in the same way as prepositions in English like "in," "on," "at," "to," and "from." While both -에 and -에서 indicate locations, each has slightly different use and meaning. Let's see how these words can be used in sentences.

Location Marker I: -에

-에 is the location marker indicating status. It is used with verbs that mean status, and can't be used with verbs that represent actions. As there aren't many Korean verbs indicating status, you can memorize the following words and use -에 when you see these verbs.

Listen to Track 185

Status verbs that can be used with -에

Verbs	Meaning
있다	*to exist / to be*
없다	*not to exist / not to be*
앉다	*to sit*
서다	*to stand*
눕다	*to lie down*

짓다	to build
살다	to live
생기다	to be created
계시다	to be (polite form)
머무르다	to stay

It can be confusing as Korean verbs indicating status can be verbs indicating action in English. If you are confused, you can see if you can do those actions continuously to stay in that status. Let's see some examples!

Listen to Track 186

- 앉다 *(to sit)* : you sit once to enter the status of sitting.
  나는 벤치**에** 앉았다. *(I sat on the bench.)*

- 서다 *(to stand)*: you stand once to enter the status of standing.
  고양이가 내 머리 위**에** 섰다. *(The cat stood on my head.)*

- 짓다 *(to build)*: you build a house once and the house will remain in the status of "built."
  나는 마당**에** 개집을 지었다. *(I built a doghouse in my yard.)*

- 눕다 *(to lie down)*: you lie down once to enter the status of "lying."
  나는 잔디밭**에** 누웠다. *(I lay down on the grass.)*

- 생기다 *(to be created)*: when a thing is created once and stay there.
  눈 옆**에** 여드름이 생겼다. *(I got a pimple next to my eye.)*

Don't worry if you don't understand it right now. It can be tricky to say which ones are status-indicating verbs. Luckily, there aren't many Korean verbs indicating status, as adjectives can do the job. For now it should be enough to memorize these 10 verbs and use -에 whenever you see them!

Location Marker II: -에서

If you don't know which location particle you should use, -에서 will be the safer choice! Because -에서 is used with verbs indicating action, and most verbs indicate actions!

Listen to Track 187

Action verbs that can be used with -에서

Verbs	Meaning
읽다	*to read*
뛰다	*to run/jump*
마시다	*to drink*
자다	*to sleep*
놀다	*to play*
달리다	*to run*
보다	*to see*
살다	*to live*

Listen to Track 188

Unlike -에, verbs followed by -에서 are indicating actions which we can do continuously. Let's see some examples.

- 읽다 *(to read)*: To read is an action; you can keep reading something.
  나는 집**에서** 신문을 읽고 있다. *(I am reading newspapers **at** home.)*

- 살다 *(to live)*: You might notice 살다 (to live) can be used with both 에(E) and 에서(E-seo).
  나는 한국**에** 살고 있다. *(I live **in** Korea.)*
  It simply says I am being in Korea.

- 나는 한국**에서** 살고 있다. *(I am living **in** Korea.)*
  It indicates I am doing specific things such as working or studying.

- 자다 *(to sleep)*: 자다 (to sleep) is an action verb while 눕다 (to lie down) and 앉다 (to sit) are status verbs.
  내 강아지는 바닥**에서** 잤다. *(My dog slept **on** the floor.)*

As you can see, -에 can be used with status verbs while -에서 can be used with action verbs. It's totally okay if you are confused as the rules to define types of verbs are different in each language. Just remember -에 is about status and -에서 is about action!

Listen to Track 189

-에 and -에서 as Postpositions

There's another use for these markers. -에 and -에서 work in the same way as the English prepositions "to" and "from" do, respectively. You don't have to think about types of verbs when it means "to" and "from" as these simply work like English prepositions.

- 원숭이가 동물원**에서** 탈출했다. (*A monkey escaped **from** the zoo.*)
- 어머니가 미용실**에** 들어간다. (*My mother enters **into** the hair salon.*)
- 나는 뉴욕**에** 간다. (*I am going **to** New York.*)
- 내 친구는 서울**에서** 왔다. (*My friend is **from** Seoul.*)

TIME TO PRACTICE!

Location Markers -에/-에서

Exercise 1. Fill in the blanks to complete the following sentences:

1. 나는 언덕 위 _____ 집을 지었다. *(I built a house up on the hill.)*
2. 고양이가 책상 _____ 앉아 있다. *(The cat is sitting on the desk.)*
3. 나는 도서관 _____ 공부했다. *(I studied in the library.)*
4. 지갑 _____ 돈이 없어요. *(There is no money in the wallet.)*
5. 나는 PC방 _____ 게임을 했다. *(I played video games at the PC café.)*
6. 영화관 _____ 어떤 영화를 봤어요? *(Which movie did you watch at the cinema?)*
7. 동생은 놀이터 _____ 친구들과 놀았다. *(My sister played on the playground with her friends.)*
8. 강아지가 바닥 _____ 누워 있어요. *(The puppy is lying on the floor.)*
9. 저는 바닥 _____ 주스를 쏟았어요. *(I spilled juice on the floor.)*
10. 집 _____ 낮잠을 잤어요. *(I took a nap at home.)*

Exercise 2. Choose the right word in the following sentences:

1. 저는 노래방 [에 / 에서] 노래를 불렀어요. *(I sang songs in the Noraebang [Karaoke].)*
2. 냉장고 [에 / 에서] 아이스크림이 있어요. *(There is ice cream in the fridge.)*
3. 라면 [에 / 에서] 계란을 넣었어요. *(I put an egg in Ramen.)*
4. 저는 수영장 [에 / 에서] 갈 거예요. *(I will go to the swimming pool.)*
5. 저는 내일 수영장 [에 / 에서] 수영할 거예요. *(I will go swim in the swimming pool tomorrow.)*
6. 오늘 저녁에 공원 [에 / 에서] 산책할까요? *(Shall we take a walk at the park this evening?)*
7. 내 누나는 한국 [에 / 에서] 가고 싶어 한다. *(My sister wants to visit Korea.)*
8. 거리 [에 / 에서] 길거리 예술가가 있다. *(There is a street artist on the street.)*
9. 어제 내 방 [에 / 에서] 귀신을 봤어! *(I saw a ghost in my room yesterday!)*
10. 거기 [에 / 에서] 사무실까지 오는데 얼마나 걸려요? *(How long does it take from there to the office?)*

Exercise 3. Determine if the following sentences are Correct / Incorrect:

1. 저는 내년에 독일에 갈 거예요. [Correct / Incorrect]
   I will go to Germany next year.

2. 친구가 의자에서 앉았어요. [Correct / Incorrect]
   My friend sat on the chair.

3. 어디에서 시끄러운 소리가 나는 거지? [Correct / Incorrect]
   Where is the noise coming from?

4. 어제 밤에 어디에 있었어? [Correct / Incorrect]
   Where were you last night?

5. 신나는 음악에 맞춰 같이 춤을 추자! [Correct / Incorrect]
   Let's dance to this music together!

6. 가방에서 무엇이 들어 있어요? [Correct / Incorrect]
   What is in the bag?

7. 화재는 부엌에 시작되었다. [Correct / Incorrect]
   The fire started in the kitchen.

8. 다시 학교에서 가고 싶다. [Correct / Incorrect]
   I want to go to school again.

9. 해변에서 같이 놀자! [Correct / Incorrect]
   Let's hang out on the beach!

10. 학교에 집으로 오는 길이다. [Correct / Incorrect]
    I am on my way home from school.

Exercise 4. Determine if the following Korean verbs are Status / Action verbs:

1. 머무르다(To stay): [Status verb / Action verb]
2. 있다(To exist/To be): [Status verb / Action verb]
3. 놀다(To play): [Status verb / Action verb]
4. 뛰다(To run/To jump): [Status verb / Action verb]
5. 마시다(To drink): [Status verb / Action verb]
6. 달리다(To run): [Status verb / Action verb]
7. 짓다(To build): [Status verb / Action verb]
8. 없다(Not to exist/Not to be): [Status verb / Action verb]
9. 보다(To see): [Status verb / Action verb]
10. 앉다(To sit) [Status verb / Action verb]

Exercise 5. Determine if the following statements are True / False:

1. "에" can be used with action verbs. [True / False]
2. The postposition "에" means the preposition "to" in English. [True / False]
3. "에서" can be used with adjectives. [True / False]
4. "에서" and "에" should be connected to a noun to indicate a location. [True / False]
5. To mean the preposition "from," "에" should be used. [True / False]
6. "에" is a postposition while "에서" is a preposition. [True / False]
7. "에서" cannot be used with the verb "살다(To live)." [True / False]
8. "에" can be used with status verbs. [True / False]
9. Even if a Korean verb means an action in English, it can be a status verb. [True / False]
10. The verb "살다" can be both a status verb and an action verb. [True / False]

Exercise 6. Select the correct word to complete the sentence:

나는	식당에 / 식당에서	점심을 먹는다.
I eat lunch at the restaurant.		
고양이는	침대에 / 침대에서	자고 있다.
The cat is sleeping on the bed.		
어머니가	회사에 / 회사에서	돌아오셨다.
My mother returned from work.		
내 동생은	독일에 / 독일에서	간다.
My sister is going to Germany		
나는 친구들과	클럽에 / 클럽에서	놀았다.
I hung out with my friends in the club.		
강아지가	거리에 / 거리에서	앉아 있다.
The dog is sitting on the street.		
아버지는	시장에 / 시장에서	가셨다.
My father went to the market.		
내 오빠는	미국에 / 미국에서	일한다.
My brother works in America.		

ANSWERS:

Exercise 1

1. 에 / 2. 에 / 3. 에서 / 4. 에 / 5. 에서 / 6. 에서 / 7. 에서 / 8. 에 / 9. 에 / 10. 에서

Exercise 2

1. 에서 / 2.에 / 3. 에 / 4. 에 / 5. 에서 / 6. 에서 / 7. 에 / 8. 에 / 9. 에서 / 10. 에서

Exercise 3

1. Correct / 2. Incorrect: "에" should be used as "앉다(To sit)" is a status verb. / 3. Correct / 4. Correct / 5. Correct / 6. Incorrect: "에" should be used as "있다(to be)" is a status verb. / 7. Incorrect: "에서" should be used as "시작하다(To start)" is an action verb. / 8. Incorrect: "에" should be used to mean the preposition "to." / 9. Correct / 10. Incorrect: "에서" should be used to mean the postposition "from."

Exercise 4

1. Status / 2. Status / 3. Action / 4. Action / 5. Action / 6. Action / 7. Status / 8. Status / 9. Action / 10. Status

Exercise 5

1. False: "에" can be used with adjectives and status verbs. / 2. True / 3. False: "에서" can be used with action verbs. / 4. True / 5. False: to mean the preposition "from," "에서" should be used. / 6. False: both are postpositions. / 7. False: "살다" can be used with both "에" and "에서." / 8. True / 9. True / 10. True

Exercise 6

1. 식당에서 / 2. 침대에서 / 3. 회사에서 / 4. 독일에 / 5. 클럽에서 / 6. 거리에 / 7. 시장에 / 8. 미국에서

QUICK RECAP

Today you have studied one of the trickiest grammar points in Korean. Now whenever you see -에 and -에서, you will know if the verb is a status verb or an action verb. This can be useful in studying other grammar points. Check the answer key and see if you understood the grammar perfectly. You did an excellent job today!

	-에	-에서
Meaning	In / At / On	
	To	From
After	Noun	
With	Status verb	Action verb

LESSON 20: HOW TO USE KOREAN POSTPOSITIONS "FROM" AND "UNTIL"

In this lesson, we are going to learn about the Korean postpositions corresponding to the English prepositions which indicate "from," "from A to B," and "until." The words -에서, -부터, and -까지 are the Korean postpositions to indicate the starting and the ending point. Let us see how we can use them in Korean sentences.

The Postposition -에서

The postposition -에서 has various functions. Among its various functions, however, the most common use for the postposition -에서 is to indicate the range of time and space or sources of something. It works in a similar way as the English preposition "from."

How to Use the Postposition -에서

1) To indicate the starting point

Listen to Track 190

Firstly, we can use the postposition -에서 to indicate starting points. Since -에서 can be used with nouns or pronouns, you can just put -에서 after nouns or pronouns without finding verb stems or adjectives or transforming verbs into basic forms.

- 서울**에서** 몇 시에 출발할 예정이에요? *(When will you depart from Seoul?)*
  → 서울 (Noun) + 에서 (Postposition) = 서울에서 (Adverb) / from Seoul
  → The postposition 에서 can indicate the starting point for traveling or a journey.

- 그 회사는 자동차**에서** 칫솔에 이르기까지 다양한 상품을 수출한다. *(The company exports various goods from automobiles to toothbrushes.)*
  → 자동차 (Noun) + 에서 (Postposition) = 자동차에서 (Adverb) / from automobiles
  → -에서 can also indicate the starting point for a range of products.

- 집**에서** 학교까지 가는 데 얼마나 걸려요**?** *(How long does it take from home to the school?)*
  - → 집 (Noun) + 에서 (Postposition) = 집에서 (Adverb) / from home
  - → You can use -에서 when it means "from the starting point."

2) To indicate sources of something

Secondly, the -에서 can also means sources of something such as money. You can put the -에서 after nouns or pronouns.

Listen to Track 191

- 그는 회사**에서** 뇌물을 받아서 감옥에 있다. *(He is in prison as he took bribes from the company.)*
  - → 회사 (Noun) + 에서 (Postposition) = 회사에서 (Adverb) / from the company
  - → You can indicate the source of the bribes using -에서.

- 그는 자기 책이 팔릴 때마다 출판사**에서** 인세를 받는다. *(He gets royalties from the publisher for every book sold.)*
  - → 출판사 (Noun) + 에서 (Postposition) = 출판사에서 (Adverb) / from the publisher
  - → You can indicate the source of the royalties using -에서.

- 그는 전국 대회**에서** "최고의 예술가" 상을 받았다. *(He won the "best artist" award from the national contest.)*
  - → 대회 (Noun) + 에서 (Postposition) = 대회에서 (Adverb) / from the national contest
  - → You can also indicate the source of an award using -에서.

3) To indicate reasons or intentions

Thirdly, you can also indicate reasons or intentions for something. You can put -에서 after nouns or pronouns.

Listen to Track 192

- 고마운 마음**에서** 드리는 말씀입니다. *(These are words from a grateful heart.) (These are words of gratitude.)*
  - → 마음 (Noun) + 에서 (Postposition) = 고마운 마음에서 (Adverb) / from gratitude
  - → You can say you are speaking to thank someone using -에서.

- 그가 도움이 되려는 뜻**에서** 한 일이다. *(He did it with the intention to be helpful.) (He meant to be helpful.)*

  → 도움이 되려는 뜻 (Noun) + 에서 (Postposition) = 도움이 되려는 뜻애서 (Adverb)

  → "도움이 되려는" is an adjective meaning "to be helpful," and "뜻" is a noun meaning "intention." Thus, you can use the postposition -에서 to indicate someone did something to be helpful.

- 우울한 마음**에서** 생긴 병이다. *(It is a disease generated from depression.)*

  → 마음 (Noun) + 에서 (Postposition) = 우울한 마음에서 (Adverb) / from depression

  → You can also indicate reasons for symptoms or diseases using -에서.

The Postposition -부터

Listen to Track 193

How to Use the Postposition 부터

1) To indicate when something starts

Both the postposition -부터 and the postposition -에서 have the same function, to indicate starting points. The postposition -부터, however, indicates the point *when* something starts, while the postposition -에서 indicates the point *where* something starts.

- 1시**부터** 5시까지 *(From 1 pm to 5 pm.)*

  → 1시 (Noun) + 부터 (Postposition) = 1시부터 / from 1 pm

  → You can indicate the starting time using -부터.

- 너**부터** 먼저 먹어라. *(You try (eat) it first.)*

  → 너 (Pronoun) + 부터 (Postposition) = 너부터 (Adverb)

  → -부터 can mean "starting from," or "first" in English.

- 그녀는 중학교**부터** 유명했다. *(She has been famous since she was in middle school.)*

  → 중학교 (Noun) + 부터 (Postposition) = 중학교부터 (Adverb)

  → -부터 can also mean "since" in English.

The Postposition -에서부터

Listen to Track 194

1) How to Use the Postposition -에서부터

To indicate either the starting time or the starting point

When you combine the two postposition -에서 and -부터, it becomes the postposition -에서부터. This postposition can indicate either the starting time or the starting point.

> **Note:** *The postposition 에서부터 can be used interchangeably with the postposition 에서 or 부터 only when it indicates the starting time **or** point. You might want to practice using the postpositions 에서 and 부터 first so that you can fully understand the differences between the two words before using -에서부터!*

- 한 시**에서부터** 두 시 사이까지 전화가 올 것이다. *(We will get calls from 1 pm to 2 pm.)*
  → 한 시 (Noun) + 에서부터 (Postposition) = 한 시에서부터 (Adverb) / from 1 pm
  → -에서부터 can indicate the starting time.

- 여기**에서부터** 세 시간은 걸린다. *(It takes 3 hours to get there from here.)*
  → 여기 (pronoun) + 에서부터 (Postposition) = 여기에서부터 (Adverb) / from here
  → -에서부터 can indicate the starting point.

- 서울**에서부터** 부산까지 가는 것은 피곤하다. *(It is tiring to go to Busan from Seoul.)*
  → 서울 (Noun) + 에서부터 (Postposition) = 서울에서부터 (Adverb) / from Seoul
  → -에서부터 can indicate the starting place.

The Postposition -까지

The postposition -까지 means "until," "by," or "to" in English. It can be used alone, or with other postpositions indicating the starting time or point such as -에서, -부터, and -에서부터.

Note: The phrase 머리부터 발끝까지 ("from head to toe") is a good one to learn, because not only will it help you remember the usage of 부터 and 까지, but also because it is frequently used in many K-pop songs, such as Hormone War by BTS, Hot Issue by 4Minute, and Fantastic Baby by Big Bang.

How to use the postposition 까지

1) To mean "to"

Listen to Track 195

- 오늘은 영어 알파벳 **A부터 Z까지** 공부할 거예요. *(Today I will study the English alphabet from A to Z.)*
  → Z (Noun) + 까지 (Postposition) = Z까지 (Adverb) / to Z
  → You can indicate the ending point using -까지.

- 지구**에서부터** 달**까지**의 거리. *(The distance from the earth to the moon.)*
  → 달 (Noun) + 까지 (Postposition) = 달까지 (Adverb) / to the moon
  → You can indicate the ending point using -까지.

- 누나는 나를 공항**까지** 데려다 주었다. *(My sister took me to the airport.)*
  → 공항 (Noun) + 까지 (Postposition) = 공항까지 (Adverb) / to the airport.
  → You can use -까지 when you take someone to an airport, a harbor, or a station.

2) To mean "until" or "by"

Listen to Track 196

- 모든 일이 끝날 때**까지** 포기하지 않을 것이다. *(We will not give up until we complete all tasks.)*
  → 때 (Noun) + 까지 (Postposition) = 때까지 (adverb) / until
  → -까지 can mean "until" in English.

- 내일은 8시**까지** 회사에 출근해야 한다. *(I have to arrive at work by 8 pm tomorrow.)*
  → 8시 (Noun) + 까지 (Postposition) = 8시까지 (adverb) / by 8 pm
  → -까지 can mean "by" in English.

- 오늘 저녁 9시**까지** 숙제를 제출해주세요. *(Please submit your assignment by 9 pm today.)*
  → 9시 (Noun) + 까지 (Postposition) = 9시까지 (adverb) / by 9 pm
  → -까지 can also refer to deadlines.

TIME TO PRACTICE!

How to Use Korean Postpositions "from" and "until"

Exercise 1. Find the right position to put 에서:

1. ① 서울 ② 몇 ③ 시에 ④ 출발할 ⑤ 예정이니 ⑥?
   (When will you depart from Seoul?) _____

2. ① 그는 ② 회사 ③ 뇌물을 ④ 받아서 ⑤ 감옥에 ⑥ 있다 ⑦.
   (He is in prison for taking bribes from a company.) _____

3. ① 고마운 ② 마음 ③ 드리는 ④ 말씀입니다 ⑤.
   (These are words of gratitude.) _____

4. ① 도움이 ② 되고 ③ 싶은 ④ 마음 ⑤ 한 ⑥ 일이다 ⑦.
   (I did it because I wanted to help you.) _____

5. ① 수업 ② 시간은 ③ 한 ④ 시 ⑤ 두시까지이다 ⑥.
   (The class is from 1 pm to 2 pm.) _____

6. ① 나는② 지금 ③ 학교 ④ 집으로 ⑤ 돌아왔다 ⑥.
   (I just arrived home from school.) _____

7. ① 서울 ② 부산까지는 ③ 5시간 ④ 정도 ⑤ 걸린다 ⑥.
   (It takes about 5 hours from Seoul to Busan.) _____

8. ① 집 ② 지하철역까지 ③ 얼마나 ④ 걸리나요 ⑤?
   (How long does it take from the subway station to home?) _____

9. ① 여기 ② 지갑을 ③ 잃어버렸다 ④. *(I lost a wallet here.)* _____

10. ① 동생이 ② 체코 ③ 돌아왔다 ④.
    (My sister came back from the Czech Republic.) _____

Exercise 2: Find the right position to put 부터 or 까지:

1. ① 점심시간은 ② 한 ③ 시 ④ 두 ⑤ 시까지이다 ⑥.
   (Lunchtime is from 1 pm to 2 pm.) _____

2. ① 너 ② 먼저 ③ 먹어라 ④. *(Eat first.)* _____

3. ① 그는 ② 초등학생때 ③ 똑똑했다 ④.
   (He has been smart since elementary school.) _____

4. ① 그녀는 ② 태어날 ③ 때 ④ 눈이 ⑤ 보이지 ⑥ 않았다 ⑦.
   (She was born blind.) _____

5. ① 오늘 ② 아침 ③ 눈이 ④ 오고 ⑤ 있다 ⑥.
   (It has been snowing since this morning.) _____

6. ① 일 ② 십 중에서 ③ 숫자를 ④ 하나 ⑤ 선택하세요 ⑥.
   (Choose a number from one to ten.) _____

7. ① 그는 ② 집에서부터 ③ 버스 ④ 정류장 ⑤ 달렸다 ⑥.
   (He ran to the bus stop from home.) _____

8. ① 누나를 ② 기차역 ③ 바래다주었다 ④.
   (I took my sister back to the train station.) _____

9. ① 내일은 ② 아침 ③ 8시 ④ 회사에 ⑤ 도착해야 ⑥ 한다 ⑦.
   (I have to arrive at work by 8 am.) _____

10. ① 저녁 ② 먹기 ③ 전 ④ 집으로 ⑤ 돌아와라 ⑥.
    (Come back home before eating dinner.) _____

Exercise 3: Fill in the blanks with the correct postpositions:

1. 나는 부산 _____ 여름방학을 보냈다. *(I spent my summer vacation in Busan.)*

2. 나는 산 _____ 캠핑을 했다. *(I camped in the mountains.)*

3. 박쥐는 동굴 _____ 산다. *(Bats live in caves.)*

4. 집에서 학교 _____ 가깝다. *(School is close to home.)*

5. 미국에서 한국 _____ 거리는 6,563 마일이다. *(The distance between America and Korea is 6,563 miles.)*

6. 버스가 없어서 학교에서 집 _____ 걸어왔다. *(I walked home as there was no bus.)*

7. 이 드론은 100 km 떨어진 곳 _____ 물건을 배달할 수 있다. *(This drone can deliver things up to 100 km away.)*

8. 기차역에서 여기 _____ 오는 데 얼마나 걸렸나요? *(How long did it take to come here from the train station?)*

9. 6시 _____ 7시까지 저녁시간이다. *(Dinner time is from 6 pm to 7 pm.)*

10. 이제 _____ 공부에 집중하자. *(Let us focus on studying from now on.)*

Exercise 4: Determine if the following sentences are Correct / Incorrect:

1. 나는 서울부터 일을 한다. *(I work in Seoul.)* _____
2. 나는 어제부터 운동을 시작했다. *(I started working out yesterday.)* _____
3. 나는 오늘 회사에서 월급을 받았다. *(I got my salary from my company.)* _____
4. 나는 부산에서 서울부터 비행기를 탔다. *(I took a plane from Busan to Seoul.)* _____
5. 나는 내일 아침 9시까지 회사부터 출근해야 한다. *(I have to arrive at work by 9 am tomorrow.)* _____
6. 나는 아침부터 공부하는 중이다. *(I am studying this morning.)* _____
7. 아버지는 올해부터 금연하신다고 말했다. *(My father decided to quit smoking this year).* _____
8. 어머니는 집에서 일한다. *(My mother works from home.)* _____
9. 고양이가 상자까지 나왔다. *(A cat came out of the box.)* _____
10. 나는 어제 밤 늦게부터 게임을 했다. *(I played video games until late at night.)* _____

Exercise 5: Choose the right postposition in the following sentences.

1. 새가 나무 [에서 / 부터 / 까지] 떨어졌다. *(A bird fell from the tree.)* _____
2. 지갑 [에서 / 부터 / 까지] 신용카드를 꺼냈다. *(I took my credit card out of my wallet.)* _____
3. 한국에서 프랑스 [에서 / 부터 / 까지] 얼마나 걸리나요? *(How long does it take from France to Korea?)* _____
4. 나는 냉장고 [에서 / 부터 / 까지] 주스를 꺼냈다. *(I took a bottle of juice out of the refrigerator.)* _____
5. 상자 [에서 / 부터 / 까지] 사과를 하나 꺼내라. *(Take an apple out of the box.)* _____
6. 나는 집 [에서 / 부터 / 까지] 공원까지 달렸다. *(I ran to the park from home.)* _____
7. 동생은 늦은 아침 [에서 / 부터 / 까지] 잤다. *(My brother slept until the late morning.)* _____
8. 어제 아버지는 밤 [에서 / 부터 / 까지] 일했다. *(Yesterday, my father worked until night time.)* _____
9. 다음 달 [에서 / 부터 / 까지] 휴가입니다. *(I am on vacation until next month.)* _____
10. 나는 오늘 아침 [에서 / 부터 / 까지] 한국어 공부를 하고 있다. *(I have been studying Korean since this morning.)* _____

ANSWERS:

Exercise 1

1. ② / 2. ③ / 3. ③ / 4. ⑤ / 5. ⑤ / 6. ④ / 7. ② / 8. ② / 9. ② /10. ③

Exercise 2

1. ④ / 2. ② / 3. ③ / 4. ④ / 5. ③ / 6. ② / 7. ③ / 8. ③ / 9. ④ / 10. ④

Exercise 3

1. 에서 / 2. 에서 / 3. 에 / 4. 까지 / 5. 까지 / 6. 까지 / 7. 까지 / 8. 까지 / 9. 부터 / 10. 부터

Exercise 4

1. Incorrect (서울부터 -> 서울에서) / 2. Correct / 3. Correct / 4. Incorrect (서울부터 -> 서울까지) / 5. Correct / 6. Correct / 7. Correct / 8. Correct / 9. Incorrect (상자까지 -> 상자에서) / 10. Incorrect (늦게부터 -> 늦게까지)

Exercise 5

1. 에서 / 2. 에서 / 3. 까지 / 4. 에서 / 5. 에서 / 6. 에서 / 7. 까지 / 8. 까지 / 9. 까지 / 10. 부터

QUICK RECAP

You learned about four Korean postpositions to indicate starting points and ending points. It will be useful to practice these postpositions, since words like "from," "to," "until," and "since" are frequently used both in Korean and English. You did an amazing job today!

	-에서	-부터	-에서부터	-까지
After	A noun or a pronoun			
Using	-에서	-부터	-에서부터	-까지
Meaning	From	From / Since		To / By
	Starting point; Source of something; Intentions; Reasons	Starting time	Starting point; Starting time	Ending point; Deadlines

LESSON 21: HOW TO MAKE AN IMPERATIVE SENTENCE

In this lesson, we will learn about how to make an imperative sentence in Korean. Imperatives are used to give commands, requests, orders, or warnings. While English omits a subject and places a verb at the beginning of a sentence, Korean uses the **imperative ending -(으) 세요** to make an imperative sentence. Let us look at how we can make an imperative sentence.

The Level of Speech in Korean

If you ask a Korean what the unique feature of the Korean language is, he or she will say it is the "level of speech." What is the level of speech? Let's see an English example first.

- Do it.
- Please do it.
- Could you please do it?
- Would it be possible for you to do it?

While the four sentences have the same meaning, the level of speech of each sentence is different, and different levels of speech are needed for different situations. For example, if you say "Do it" to your teacher or boss, you might get into trouble.

In Korean, the level of speech is more important and complicated. First, you have to check if the conversation needs formality, and then you choose the degree of politeness. If you talk to your friends, for example, you speak in an informal and "impolite" way. If you talk to your boss, you speak formally and politely.

There are six imperative endings in modern Korean. Using proper endings for every situation is not easy, even for Koreans. Don't worry, however, since we are going to learn the most popular ending -(으)세요 today.

Imperative Ending -(으)세요

Listen to Track 197

	Formal		Informal	
Honorific	Most Polite	하십시오	Polite	(으)세요 / 해요
	Less Polite	하오		
Non-Honorific	Less Impolite	하게	Impolite	해
	Most Impolite	해라		

The Imperative ending -(으)세요 lies between the most polite and formal ending "하십시오," and polite and informal ending "해요." Although -(으)세요 is an informal ending, it is widely used in various situations these days.

As it is polite but not too formal, the imperative ending -(으)세요 is useful when you are not fluent in Korean. Let's see how we can use it.

How to use the ending -(으)세요

As you can guess from its name, you can put the imperative ending -(으)세요 at the end of a sentence. The difference is that this time you have to check not only if there is a final consonant but also if the final consonant is "ㄹ."

	-으세요	-세요
After	An infinitive of a verb	
Condition	The infinitive ends **with a final consonant** (except for "ㄹ")	The infinitive ends **with a vowel** or with "ㄹ."

Although the level of speech and grammar of the imperative endings can be tricky, using it is simple and straightforward. Let's look at how we can use it in sentences.

1) To transform a verb into an imperative sentence

You can transform a verb into an imperative sentence. Find an infinitive of a verb and connect it to the imperative ending -(으)세요.

- 가다. -> **가세요**. *(to go -> Go, please.)*

  Since the verb stem 가- of 가다 has no final consonant, you have to use -세요.

  The verb "가다" becomes an imperative sentence.

- 앉다. -> **앉으세요**. *(to sit -> Please sit down.)*

  As the verb stem 앉- of 앉다 has a final consonant and it is not "ㄹ," you have to use -으세요.

  The verb "앉다" becomes an imperative sentence.

2) To transform a sentence into an imperative sentence

You can transform a sentence into an imperative sentence. Find the infinitive of the verb and replace the original ending with the imperative ending -(으)세요.

Listen to Track 199

- 모두 자리에서 **일어나다**. -> 모두 자리에서 **일어나세요**. *(Everyone stands up. -> Please stand up, everyone.)*

  As the verb stem 일어나- of 일어나다 has no final consonant, you have to use -세요.

  The declarative sentence becomes an imperative sentence.

- 증인은 신중하게 **대답한다**. -> 증인은 신중하게 **대답하세요**. *(The witness answers carefully. -> (To the witness) You must answer carefully.)*

  As the verb stem 대답하- of 대답하다 has no final consonant, you have to use -세요.

  The declarative sentence becomes an imperative sentence.

TIME TO PRACTICE!

How to Make an Imperative Sentence

Exercise 1. Transform the verb into an imperative sentence:

1. 가다 -> _____. (To go -> Go, please.)
2. 먹다 -> _____. (To eat -> Eat it, please.)
3. 쉬다 -> _____. (To rest. -> Take a rest, please.)
4. 오다 -> _____. (To come -> Please come here.)
5. 일어나다 -> _____. (To stand up -> Please stand up.)
6. 앉다 -> _____. (To sit -> Please sit down.)
7. 말하다 -> _____. (To speak -> Please speak.)
8. 쓰다 -> _____. (To write -> Please write it down.)
9. 가져가다 -> _____. (To take -> Please take it.)
10. 보관하다 -> _____. (To keep -> Please keep it.)

Exercise 2. Transform the following into imperative sentences:

1. 너는 점심을 먹다. -> 점심을 _____.
   (You have lunch. -> Have lunch, please.)

2. 모두 앉다. -> 모두 _____.
   (Everyone sits. -> Please sit down, everyone.)

3. 너는 오렌지 주스를 마시다. -> 오렌지 주스를 _____.
   (You drink a glass of orange juice. -> Drink a glass of orange juice, please.)

4. 모두 잠시 쉬다. -> 모두 잠시 _____.
   (Everyone takes a rest. -> Please take a rest, everyone.)

5. 너는 한국어 공부를 하다. -> 한국어 공부를 _____.
   (You study Korean. -> Study Korean, please.)

6. 너는 손을 내리다. -> 손을 _____.
   (You lower your hand. -> Please lower your hand.)

7. 모두 눈을 감다. -> 모두 눈을 _____.
   (Everyone closes their eyes. -> Please close your eyes.)

8. 너는 여기로 오다. -> 여기로 _____.
   (You come here. -> Please come here.)

9. 너는 우산을 가져가다. -> 우산을 _____.
   (You take an umbrella -> Please take an umbrella.)

10. 너는 왜 늦었는지 설명하다. -> 왜 늦었는지 _____.
    (You explain why you are late. -> Please explain why you are late.)

Exercise 3. Choose the correct word inside the bracket to complete the sentences:

1. 아침을 먹 [세요 / 으세요]. *(Eat breakfast, please.)* _____
2. 커피를 한 잔 마시 [세요 / 으세요]. *(Drink a cup of coffee, please.)* _____
3. 휴대폰을 끄 [세요 / 으세요]. *(Please turn off your phone.)* _____
4. 매일 운동을 하 [세요 / 으세요]. *(Please exercise every day.)* _____
5. 영어 공부를 하 [세요 / 으세요]. *(Please study English.)* _____
6. 잠을 푹 자 [세요 / 으세요]. *(Please get enough sleep.)* _____
7. 노래를 한 곡 부르 [세요 / 으세요]. *(Please sing a song.)* _____
8. 그 책을 가져오 [세요 / 으세요]. *(Please bring that book.)* _____
9. 이 문서를 챙기 [세요 / 으세요]. *(Please take this document.)* _____
10. 여기 앉 [세요 / 으세요]. *(Please sit here.)* _____

Exercise 4. Determine if the following sentences are Correct / Incorrect:

1. 피자 하나 주으세요. *(One pizza, please.)* _____
2. 저 것을 보세요. *(Please look at that.)* _____
3. 공항으로 가주세요. *(Please go to the airport.)* _____
4. 일어서으세요. *(Please stand up.)* _____
5. 손을 드세요. *(Please raise your hand.)* _____
6. 모두 조용히 해주세요. *(Please be quiet.)* _____
7. 콜라 하나 주세요. *(One cola, please.)* _____
8. 모두 여기 앉세요. *(Please sit here, everyone.)* _____
9. 모자를 벗세요. *(Please take off your hat.)* _____
10. 신발을 신으세요. *(Please put on your shoes.)* _____

Exercise 5. Check if the following statements are True / False:

1. The imperative ending (으)세요 is an informal ending. _____
2. The imperative ending (으)세요 is an impolite ending. _____
3. It is okay to use any imperative endings. _____
4. The imperative ending 하십시오 is an informal ending. _____

5. When the bottom character of an infinitive is "ㄴ," you have to use 으세요. _____

6. There are 12 imperative endings in Korean. _____

7. You can use both 세요 and 으세요 after an infinitive of a verb. _____

8. When the bottom consonant of an infinitive is "ㄹ," you have to use 세요. _____

9. You can transform a sentence into an imperative sentence. _____

10. When an infinitive has no bottom consonant, you have to use 으세요. _____

ANSWERS

Exercise 1

1. 가세요 / 2. 먹으세요 / 3. 쉬세요 / 4. 오세요 / 5. 일어나세요 / 6. 앉으세요 /
7. 말하세요 / 8. 쓰세요 / 9. 가져가세요 / 10. 보관하세요

Exercise 2

1. 먹으세요 / 2. 앉으세요 / 3. 마시세요 / 4. 쉬세요 / 5. 하세요 / 6. 내리세요 /
7. 감으세요 / 8. 오세요 / 9. 가져가세요 / 10. 설명하세요

Exercise 3

1. 으세요 / 2. 세요 / 3. 세요 / 4. 세요 / 5. 세요 / 6. 세요 / 7. 세요 / 8. 세요 /
9. 세요 / 10. 으세요.

Exercise 4

1. Incorrect (주으세요 -> 주세요) / 2. Correct / 3. Correct / 4. Incorrect
(일어서으세요 -> 일어서세요) / 5. Correct / 6. Correct / 7. Correct /
8. Incorrect (앉세요 -> 앉으세요) / 9. Incorrect (벗세요 -> 벗으세요) /
10. Correct

Exercise 5

1. True / 2. False ("(으)세요" is a polite ending.) / 3. False (It is important to
use proper imperative endings for different situations.) / 4. False ("하십시오"
is a formal ending.) / 5. True / 6. False (There are six imperative endings.) /
7. False (You can use "으세요" when an infinitive of a verb ends with a bottom
consonant.) / 8. False (you have to use "으세요" when the bottom consonant
of an infinitive is "ㄹ.") / 9. True / 10. False (You have to use "세요" when an
infinitive has no bottom consonant.)

QUICK RECAP

In this final lesson, you learned about the imperative ending - (으)세요. We only went over a polite ending in detail, but please make note of the types of the level of speech in Korean. They will come in handy as you get further along in your learning journey. You did an excellent job today, and throughout all these lessons!

	-으세요	세요
After	An infinitive of a verb	
Condition	The infinitive ends **with a bottom character** (except for "ㄹ")	The infinitive ends **without a bottom character** or with "ㄹ."

CONCLUSION

Learning grammar is never an easy task so if you were able to finish all the lessons in this book by consistently learning every day, kudos to you! You did an amazing job and you should be very happy with your achievement.

If you were not able to follow the daily schedules as recommended, don't despair. The important thing is you made use of this book to build a solid foundation for your Korean grammar. We at Fluent in Korean hope that you will continue learning every day.

Even just an hour or less a day will go a long way. It could be just listening to a 30-minute Korean podcast, watching a Korean movie or TV series, writing to a friend in Korean, talking to a native Korean speaker, changing your social media settings to Korean or reading the news in Korean.

If you wish to further your studies in Korean language, we have other books available at FluentinKorean.com and on Amazon. Please feel free to browse the different titles. The books, such as Korean Short Stories, will help improve your reading and listening skills as well as solidify the knowledge you learned in this grammar book.

Thank you for sticking with us all the way to the end! We hope you got a lot out of this book! We'd love to hear what you think. If you have comments, questions, or suggestions about this book, please let us know by sending us an email at support@ fluentinkorean.com. This will help us to enhance our books and provide you with better learning resources.

It has been a great 21 days (or more) with you. We wish you the best of luck in your Korean studies.

Thank you,

Fluent in Korean Team

ENGLISH-KOREAN GLOSSARY

조금	a bit	커피	coffee
미리	ahead of time	계속	continuously
벌써	already	과자	cookie
이미	already	시원하다	cool
항상	always	오이	cucumber
그리고	and	컵	cup
사과	apple	의사	doctor
이모	aunt	각	each
곰	bear	과일	fruit
벌	bee	귀	ear
소고기	beef	일찍	early
띠	belt	여덟	eight
크다	big	여든	eighty
그런데	but	충분히	enough
차	car	눈	eye
치즈	cheese	얼굴	face
턱	chin	멀리	far
가까이	close	아빠	father
쉰	fifty	월요일	Monday
다섯	five	엄마	mother
넷	four	입	mouth
마흔	fourty	아홉	nine
금요일	Friday	아흔	ninety
금	gold	코	nose

포도	grape	코	nose
털	hair	전혀	not at all
반	half	별로	not really
머리	head	자주	often
어떻게	how	오빠	older brother (by a female)
칼	knife	형	older brother (by a male)
다리	leg	누나	older sister (by a male)
덜	less	언니	older sister (by a female)
사자	lion	하나	one
입술	lips	돼지고기	pork
간	liver	값	price
길다	long	빨리	quickly
폐	lung	정말	really
많이	many	진짜	really
고기	meat	자꾸	repeatedly
우유	milk	토요일	Saturday
적당히	moderately	일곱	seven
일흔	seventy	짓다	to build
구두	shoes	오다	to come
가수	singer	하다	to do
여섯	six	먹다	to eat
예순	sixty	가다	to go
천천히	slowly	있다	to have
작다	small	눕다	to lay down
그래서	so	살다	to live
가끔	sometimes	아니다	to not be
넋	soul	없다	to not have

아직	still, yet	읽다	to read
일요일	Sunday	머무르다	to remain
열	ten	보다	to see
서른	thirty	계시다	to stay
셋	three	두부	tofu
목요일	Thursday	화요일	Tuesday
시간	time	스물	twenty
이다	to be	둘	two
나쁘다	to be bad	너무	very
춥다	to be cold	아주	very, extremely
생기다	to be formed	따뜻하다	warm
좋다	to be good	수요일	Wednesday
덥다	to be hot	뭐	what
언제	when	왜	why
어디	where	남동생	younger brother
누구	who	동생	younger sibling

APPENDIX-SOUND CHANGE RULES

You've learned how to read Hangul, but now let's go over a few rules regarding sound changes that take place between syllables.

The sound change rules shown here in this appendix are not needed when pronouncing a word slowly, one syllable at a time, but when Korean is spoken at a natural pace, these rules apply.

These rules will take a bit of time to master, so don't worry about memorizing them the first time you read them. When speaking in Korean and applying these pronunciation rules, try speaking slowly at first then increasing your speed as you get used to the pronunciation.

Rule 1: Consonant + Base Consonant

First let's talk about base consonants: ㄱ, ㄷ, ㅂ, ㅅ, ㅈ. These five consonants are the basis for learning sound change rules in Korean. Memorize these five letters. Now let's jump into the first sound change rule!

This rule is used anytime we have a consonant that is used right before a base consonant. When this happens, the second consonant is pronounced like a double consonant, making it more tense.

Examples:

- 잡지 → 잡찌
- 먹다 → 먹따
- 받다 → 받따
- 찾다 → 찬따

Rule 2: Re-syllabification

This rule is used when the first character ends with a consonant and the next character starts with a vowel. When this happens, the bottom consonant of the first syllable block gets carried over to the second syllable block. The only exception is if the first syllable block ends with a ㅇ, then it isn't carried over.

Examples:

- 십일 → 시빌
- 잡아요 → 자바요
- 먹어요 → 머거요

Rule 3: ㅂ/ㅍ + ㄴ

Whenever you have a ㅂ or ㅍ at the end of a syllable block before an ㄴ at the start of the next syllable block, the ㅂ or ㅍ will be pronounced like an ㅁ. This rule is pretty simple, but practice reading the examples below to get used to it.

Examples:

- 덮는 → 덤는
- 합니다 → 함니다
- 굽는 → 굼는

Rule 4: Ending Consonants

Each consonant has its normal sound at the start of the character, but when placed at the end of a syllable block, aspirated consonants are pronounced like their simple counterparts: ㅋ is pronounced as ㄱ, ㅌ is pronounced as ㄷ, and ㅍ is pronounced as ㅂ.

The exception is when the next syllable block in the same word starts with a vowel sound, then it will be pronounced as normal.

Examples:

- 부엌 → 부억
- 끝 → 끋
- 꽃 → 꼳

Rule 5: 치 & 지

If you have ㄷ before 히, it is pronounced as 치; if you have ㅌ before 이, it is pronounced as 치; and if you have ㄷ before 이, it is pronounced as 지.

Examples:

- 같이 → 가치
- 굳이 → 굳이
- 붙이다 → 부치다

Rule 6: Nasal Sounds

This rule is something that a lot of beginners have trouble with because most Korean grammar books never seem to mention it, but it is pretty easy to learn. This rule is applied mostly when the start of the second syllable block is an ㄴ (n) or ㅁ (m), and the consonant at the end of the first syllable block with change to make the word easier to pronounce. ㄱ will change to ㅇ, ㄷ, ㅅ, and ㅈ will change to ㄴ, and ㅂ will change to ㅁ.

Examples:

- 국내 → 궁내
- 합니다 → 함니다
- 막내 → 망내
- 합니다 → 함니다
- 맞는 → 만는

These rules cover all of the common Korean pronunciation changes, but there are a few obscure ones out there that aren't as common. Remember: not all Korean words follow these pronunciation rules, but the vast majority of them do! There are a few irregular words that don't follow these rules, but they are best memorized on their own. Just learn the irregular words as they pop up, and don't stress about memorizing them all at once.

HOW TO DOWNLOAD THE FREE AUDIO FILES

The audio files need to be accessed online. No worries though—it's easy!

On your computer, smartphone, iPhone/iPad, or tablet, simply go to this link:

https://fluentinkorean.com/grammar-beginner/

Be careful! If you are going to type the URL on your browser, please make sure to enter it completely and exactly. Otherwise, it will lead you to an incorrect web page.

You should be directed to a web page where you can see the cover of your book.

Below the cover, you will find two "Click here to download the audio" buttons in blue and orange color.

Option 1 (via Google Drive): The blue one will take you to a Google Drive folder. It will allow you to listen to the audio files online or download them from there. Just "Right click" on the track and click "Download." You can also download all the tracks in one click—just look for the "Download all" option.

Option 2 (direct download): The orange button/backup link will allow you to directly download all the files (in .zip format) to your computer.

Note: This is a large file. Do not open it until your browser tells you that it has completed the download successfully (usually a few minutes on a broadband connection, but if your connection is slow it could take longer).

The .zip file will be found in your "Downloads" folder unless you have changed your settings. Extract the .zip file and you will now see all the audio tracks. Save them to your preferred folder or copy them to your other devices. Please play the audio files using a music/Mp3 application.

Did you have any problems downloading the audio? If you did, feel free to send an email to support@fluentinkorean.com. We'll do our best to assist you, but we would greatly appreciate it if you could thoroughly review the instructions first.

Thank you,

Fluent in Korean Team

ABOUT THE AUTHOR

FluentinKorean.com believes that Korean can be learned almost painlessly with the help of a learning habit. Through its website and the books and audiobooks that it offers, Korean language learners are treated to high-quality materials that are designed to keep them motivated until they reach their language learning goals. Keep learning Korean and enjoy the learning process with books and audio from Fluent in Korean.

FluentinKorean.com is a website created to help busy learners learn Korean. It is designed to provide a fun and fresh take on learning Korean through:

- Helping you create a daily learning habit that you will stick to until you reach fluency, and
- Making learning Korean as enjoyable as possible for people of all ages.

With the help of awesome content and tried-and-tested language learning methods, Fluent in Korean aims to be the best place on the web to learn Korean.

The website is continuously updated with free resources and useful materials to help you learn Korean. This includes grammar and vocabulary lessons plus culture topics to help you thrive in a Korean-speaking location—perfect not only for those who wish to learn Korean but also for travelers planning to visit Korean-speaking destinations.

For any questions, please email support@fluentinkorean.com.

YOUR OPINION COUNTS!

If you enjoyed this book, please consider leaving a review on Amazon and help other language learners discover it.

Scan the QR code below:

OR

 Visit the link below:

https://geni.us/DXAIx

Thank you so much.

Made in the USA
Middletown, DE
02 July 2023

34465930R00130